MID-LIFE ~~CRISIS~~ RETIREMENT

D1132540

STEPHEN RENAULT

WITH LISA DOWER

ISBN: 1502440016
ISBN 13: 9781502440013

middleretirement.com

DEDICATION

To my wife, Lisa, for her unconditional love and patience. To my children, Brandon, Heather, Caleb, Joshua and Levi, of whom I am extremely proud. And my parents for all they gave.

Nobody can go back and start a new beginning, but anyone can start today and make a new ending.—Maria Robinson

I hope this book gives you the power to understand what you have and to start your new ending.—Steve Renault

CONTENTS

INTRODUCTION:

THE NEW ENDING

To make an end is to make a beginning. The end is where we start from.—T. S. Eliot

Rain jackets? Check. School books? Check. Six pairs of jeans? Let's try two. Bread maker? Definitely not. That was the conversation in our house during summer 2002 as we attempted to fit the contents of a six-thousand-square-foot house, along with my forty-year-old self, my wife, our five kids, and our dog, into a thirty-foot travel trailer. More important, why?

The plan was to leave a high-paying job, family, friends, a beautiful house, and a booming city to hit the open road. It seemed crazy. And there was no shortage of coworkers, friends, and family to tell us exactly that.

As an owner, partner, and director of trading at a brokerage firm, I spent my days making calls to some of the world's largest fund managers. Every day, I handled trades amounting to millions of dollars, all in the blink of an eye. I spent my nights wondering if the decisions I made would allow the seventy partners and employees to receive a healthy paycheck that month—or not. I was playing the money game with Bay Street and worried about every trade and how it would affect the firm, all the while living the high-flying career of television shows.

No surprise, though, it was taking its toll. After eighteen years as a professional trader in Toronto and finally Calgary, covering Canadian, US, and European accounts, my father's words were hitting home: "Steve, when is enough, enough?"

Life in the business, I began to realize, had become solely about making money, and there was little time or energy to enjoy it. I was so caught up in the chase that I forgot *what* the chase was for. On its own, my wealth was useless, but what I did with my wealth made me happy.

I remember one evening close to the end of my trading career. As I crested the hill in the last five minutes of the drive home, I pulled into a gas station, reclined my seat, and closed my eyes. I could not turn off the office noise, the computer screen, or the day's trade results. All I wanted to do was to get home and enjoy the Alberta sunshine and my family, but I couldn't. The chaos was trapped in my head, and the only escape was to shut down completely. I stayed in the car and slept just five minutes away from everyone and everything I loved.

Assessing my quality of life began to consume me. I'd done well; I was healthy, but I needed to slow life down or the stress would kill me. A question took hold and became the focus of late-night conversations with my wife, Lisa. Could we take a break in the middle? Could we call a life-size time-out to enjoy the days instead of just getting through them?

I wanted to change from a *life of means* to a *life of meaning*.

My situation was anything but unusual. From talking to hundreds of people and reading hundreds more articles and books, I know that most of us go through some kind of midlife or mid-career crisis. It doesn't take a stressful or high-paying job to bring it on. It simply takes year after year of doing the same thing before we all start to wonder how to bring back the joy.

I married straight out of school and started my first real job and family. With two small children and a stressful career, it wasn't long before things went wrong, and my first marriage ended.

For the next few years, I struggled in my career, struggled in my family life, and struggled to find myself. I look back now and realize I was in survival mode. But somehow I kept going, earning promotions, buying a home in the suburbs, and taking that vacation every year, whether I could afford it or not.

Publicly, I was the picture of success. Privately, I was borrowing to make ends meet. The truth: I was still in survival mode. As so often happens, my income was the biggest it had ever been, but my lifestyle was even bigger. That was when my first life wake-up call occurred: I needed financial stability.

Around that time, my wife, Lisa, came into my life. Together we found financial success in different ways that we had not thought of alone. We used our small savings to buy and renovate the ugliest house in an up-and-coming neighborhood. We made a ton of mistakes and spent many hours looking for deals and learning the hard way how to do it the right way. However, a few renovations later, we'd worked our way up to a beautiful house, a small nest egg, and no more living from paycheck to paycheck and borrowing to make ends meet.

With financial stability, I was also free to make better career choices, and that led to a partnership deal with an energy investment firm. I wouldn't have taken that chance with debt on my shoulders. But that wasn't the end of the happiness equation. I learned that debt and money were only part of the picture. On the outside, I looked like I had it all, but on the inside, I was the guy taking a nap in the parking lot, unable to leave the work stress behind.

In my first life wake-up call, I realized I needed financial stability. In my second, I realized wealth is useless on its own. It's what we do with our wealth that makes us happy. And it shouldn't take a health scare or a failed marriage for us to wake up and start enjoying life or our financial success. I believe we need to spend time looking for that personal fulfillment in order to reach our full happiness potential.

So, back to the big road trip. We took the plunge and drove into *middle retirement*. I sold my shares in the company and put a plan in motion that used the income, an annuity, along with some real estate investments, to keep us going for a few years. Those few years stretched to thirteen. We eventually traded in the thirty-foot trailer for backpacks and traveled to five continents and more than forty countries. Today I'm back at work, but instead of having the stress of trading the company's money, I'm doing what I love—helping people understand their money.

Retirement in the middle has allowed me a life envied by most. I learned that following the masses, in life and finances, doesn't work. *Being a contrarian does.*

In 1996, when we moved to Calgary from Toronto, my big-city partners discouraged the move, dismissing

Calgary as a place that would limit my career and my life-style. When we decided to trade suburban life for life in a trailer, friends and family said we were crazy. When we chose to homeschool our kids, some said it would never work—their social skills would be compromised. When we traveled to remote parts of Africa, South America, and Asia, family worried we were putting the kids in danger.

In each and every experience, we have looked back and reveled in our decisions—no regrets, no disappointments. Don't get me wrong, there were many sleepless nights full of second-guessing. I still reevaluate on a regular basis, but as we look back, we have *no regrets.*

The value of middle retirement, of swimming against the tide, has been priceless and enriching for our family. Do I have the accumulated wealth I could have had by sticking with my career fourteen years ago? Not even close. But we have what we need, and we've learned to make adjustments along the way that have helped, rather than hindered our lifestyle.

Those designer vacations became backpacking adventures complete with hostels instead of five-star hotels, and private boarding schools became homeschool. My daughter Heather's favorite saying is, "You can't change the direction of the wind, but you can adjust your sails."

That is exactly what we did, and we are all the better for it. My children, my wife, and I all have a better perspective on what really matters and where we are going.

I believe middle retirement is possible for anyone who wants it. Your version may be far different from mine. It might be thirteen months, not thirteen years. Maybe it's an extended maternity or paternity leave, time off with ailing parents, or even just an extra long vacation. Maybe it's not time off that's important to you. The concept of middle retirement is simply about having the financial freedom to do what's important in the prime of life instead of at the end of your career.

The first and toughest lesson in successfully achieving middle retirement, or any retirement, is getting over yourself. Most of us identify who we are by what we do. To make a decision to walk away from work, even for a short period of time, means you need to redefine who you are.

Middle retirement is a time-out to see who you can be in life. It's freedom in the middle to pursue what's most important to you. With the right planning, you can manage both your career and your finances. The key? Spending time today to evaluate where you are, where you want to be, and how you are going to get there.

You need to think of retirement as a door opening instead of closing. For me, it was an opportunity to see who I could be outside of the stock market instead of clinging to my market persona. Early on in my retirement, when I was wrestling with new and old career options, my wife said, "If you go back to work for your ego, I feel sorry for you. If you go back because you want to, I'm happy for you."

It took me a year back in the office to realize she was right: it was for my ego, my self-esteem. I then realized that the opportunities are endless when you are able to let go of your previous title and begin anew.

Maybe your dream is spending more time with hobbies, saving for a child's education fund, or simply having enough for a stress-free, happy retirement. Either way, the formula is quite simple: once you receive a paycheck, let the money you worked for work for you.

We all have our definitions of wealth, success, and happiness. The Basotho people of Lesotho, Africa, are some of the happiest people I've ever met. When we stayed with them in a remote village and slept in their mud hut, we learned they always carry a blanket and a pocketknife, so they can eat and sleep anywhere. The style and quality of your blanket is an indication of your level of wealth. It might take years of planning and saving to buy one of the high-quality blankets, but the Basotho people can achieve their dream, because their end goal is very clear.

The New Ending

I wrote this book to help you define your middle retirement or end goal and, more important, to show you how to reach it. When we started our financial journey, we didn't know what we would be doing today, and we made many mistakes along the way. I hope this book gives you the fortitude to make decisions early so that they can pay off sooner. You'll read things that you'll find in many books—how to pay yourself first and how to put your money to work through traditional and commonly accepted investments. But I'll also show you how to be a contrarian when it comes to managing your money and achieving your goals. And we'll talk about how to create the wealth you need by examining subjects in layperson's terms rather than in the vocabulary usually reserved for accountants and financial advisors. Things like asset allocation, annuities, insurance, and stock market intelligence may sound overwhelming, but you're in for a surprise: it's not the black magic you might think.

When I retired, and even now as I look back, I saw that the answers are in front of us: peace, enjoying the now and understanding how important it is for life, and not work to be our focus. Sleeping in that hut in Lesotho, I saw that in the executive world, I wanted something new almost every day. In the mud hut, there was nothing to want; we had it all.

Years ago during one of our annual work Christmas parties, one of my partners chased my wife and I down the hall. In an uncharacteristic question on life rather than business, he asked us, "When do you know you're with *the one*? When do you know *you're happy*?"

Our answer: "If you have to ask, then she's not the right one, and you haven't found happiness."

He was in a long-term, live-in relationship, which ended shortly afterward. When he married a few years later and started a family, I hoped he had found happiness and *the one*. On a recent evening with some old business colleagues, that conversation came back very clearly. This time, however, he was characteristically asking me about tax implications and corporate structures. Even in a social setting, the dichotomy of money replaced the need for personal interaction, and I was left wondering if the success he experienced in the business world transferred to his home life. Did the question of true happiness continue to elude him, even after all these years? It was then that it struck me: *having* the right person isn't the answer; it is *being* the right person that matters.

I hope that this book will teach you about enjoying the fruits of your labor at a time in life when you can—and inspire you to avoid waiting until it is too close to the end.

> *Life has no meaning. Each of us has meaning and we bring it to life. It is a waste of time to be asking the question when you are the answer.—Joseph Campbell*

LESSON 1:

REDEFINING YOURSELF

I can't tell where the journey will end,
but I know where to start. —Avicii

One of the hardest tasks in my life has become the best part of my life: redefining myself. I left work to become a full-time dad. It was not that I hadn't been one; if you had asked anyone else that I worked with, they would tell you that I had already put my family over my career. I was surrounded by people who put their job first. The adage was Monday to Friday was for the business, and the weekends were for family. That would have been OK if I'd had a nanny after my divorce, but I didn't. And with two small children half of the time, I wasn't going to give up the little time I did have and give it to a live-in caregiver. Of course that came with a cost to my career, but I believe there are no shortcuts in life, and this was the beginning of my contrarian approach.

I was already redefining myself as a dad and making that change from stockbroker to retiree much easier. If I never spent time with my family, except to be the cotton candy dad, retirement would not be fun. If I never went on a date night or enjoyed my wife's conversation, retirement together would not be fun. And if I neglected to develop hobbies or interests outside of the office, then, yes, I would find it very difficult to redefine myself.

In life, we need to take time for the things that are important so that they will still be important in the future. If we put only work first now, then it will only be work that we are left with when we leave. One of my partners, who had been married for more than fifteen years, grieved one night at our weekly meeting about his pending divorce. He shared he had not had a proper meal with his family for more than seven years and that he didn't spend quality time with his wife or kids. The sad part was that he missed the early years, but luckily he hadn't run out of time and could still do a complete revaluation and make changes.

As we travel through life, we need to look at ourselves holistically. Our society defines us by our career, so we struggle to find *ourselves*.

I remember one day, about a month into retirement, I left the bank after filling out forms. The drive home took me to that insecure spot of realizing I didn't have a title or even a job. Who was I? Now what? There were no meetings, no calls, and no schedule. Somehow the stock market, my clients, and coworkers had managed to move on quite easily without me. I was scared that I didn't have a plan or a purpose, but I began to see that the title was just for my sake. I had five kids who needed my attention as coach, practice mate, driver, observer, and, of course, my least favorite roles: cook and cleaner. I also began to see the possibilities right in front of me, and for once I was able to truly enjoy what I had. When the sun was shining, we could enjoy the outside; if there was fresh snow, we could head to the mountains.

When we redefine ourselves and think outside the parameters of our current life, it is also essential to look within and accept who we are.

One summer, my three youngest sons started a firewood supply business. We had an overabundance on our property, and the boys saw an opportunity to make some extra cash. I encouraged the venture and helped them set up their first go at entrepreneurship. Things went very well, and after a few deliveries, they saw their company bank account growing. However, one son, Joshua, wanted a change. He was unhappy with his current, albeit equal, share of the manual labor.

As I sat with them to help mediate their differences, I could see each personality so clearly. One son had no problem cutting, loading, unloading, and stacking the wood. He enjoyed the physical labor. Joshua, on the other hand, loved the books, setting up the bank account, making the deposits and calls, placing the ads, and caring for the clients.

It was at that point that I realized in business and life we have to be true to ourselves. We can push and work outside of our comfort zone, but it is important to look at our strengths, especially as we look at our future. In the end, they didn't really need me to work it out for them. They were happy with the new division of work.

We go to school for twelve to sixteen years (or more); we have a career and work twenty-five to thirty years. The kids move out, and now it's the golden years—retirement. But I never really planned for that! I'm a mechanic; I'm an engineer; I'm a business owner; I'm a doctor. *No.* You played that role, did that job, but it's not who you are.

When I was younger, my father would ask me what I wanted to be when I grew up. I would answer hockey player, baseball player, or lawyer. He would smile, sit back, and say, "I didn't ask you what you wanted to do; I asked you what you wanted to be."

He told me, "What you want to be is a good person, one who wants to help others, do the right things, have integrity, and be proud to look in the mirror. What you do can change at any given moment; that is changeable, but who you are is not."

The baby boomers are goal oriented, work centered, and independent. We have more experience and knowledge than any generation before; we have more access to further education, international travel, new business opportunities, and entrepreneurial choices. You can choose to remain at work or sit idle and remember how important you were, or you can move forward and reinvent yourself.

As we reach or have reached retirement, finding ourselves is a focus for many. It used to be you worked the land or ran the family business until you could work no longer. This was the Agrarian Age, when our ancestors lived in small communities and lived off the land. Then came the Industrial Age, when people moved to large cities to work and support industry, join unions, and achieve job security. Unfortunately, this can no longer be the expectation. We have left that age and are now in the Information Age. This age is only ten to twenty years old; it is young, new, and ever evolving. The world is changing, and we must change with it.

Guaranteed pensions, job security, and complacency are things of the past. We no longer control a machine that stays the same day after day. Governments change rules; corporations relocate or are taken over; machines replace us; layoffs happen; corporations close. These are all out of our control.

Very few jobs today come with the job security of the past hundred years. Unions have shrunk, governments have cut back on spending, and corporate pension plans have decreased. Today's environment changes rapidly, and stagnation is not your friend. Our education system is struggling to keep up; our students are studying geography only to realize that the borders have already changed. They are using technology that is already obsolete.

We have all heard of people who retired at sixty-five, having great lives, two kids, and steady jobs. Then they begin this new stage in life with no meaning, no reason to get up in the morning. They become depressed, get sick, and die soon after, never getting to enjoy what this stage has to offer. They could not get over their past life; they could not move on and redefine themselves. Living in the past does not a future make.

Depression rates increase in the later working years. According to the US National Health and Nutrition Examination Survey, the depression rate for the forty- to fifty-nine-year-old age bracket is almost double the rate of people in the twelve- to thirty-nine-year-old bracket! When we step back, it makes sense; it is the time of the midlife crisis. Who am I? What am I here for? What do I do now? Where am I going?

One of the best ways to have purpose is to do something for others. When you give your time, you gain a sense of self-worth, a feeling of being needed. Doing for others instills power. Whether you are a young adult, a young professional, a midlifer, someone at the end of your career, or a senior, one of the most important elements of redefining yourself is to do for others. When we reduce someone else's plight, we not only help that person, but we also see our talents and how we can make a difference. Then the next steps are very clear.

On a mission trip to a refugee camp in Turkey, my son Caleb, who was sixteen at the time, came back troubled and deeply affected by what he had seen and experienced. It was one of those times when we questioned our decision as parents. Then we talked, and while his experience had definitely changed him, I learned that it was all for good. He said, "I realized I can't change the world or solve everyone's problems, but I can make someone smile, even if it is just for a brief moment, and hopefully that makes all the difference."

Ruts are hard to get out of, yet when you find a new road, the adventure will be exhilarating. You need to learn, try, open doors, and remember that when you are ninety and on that porch swing, it is the chances you did not take that will haunt you, not the chances you took, even if you failed.

Recently, a friend of mine swam five kilometers in the Atlantic Ocean, crossing from the mainland to the closest island to raise money for mental illness. No one in her family had been affected by mental illness; she did it to support the organizer and to fulfill a lifelong dream of doing a long-distance ocean swim. At forty-six, she had never been a swimmer, but she trained twice a week for four months. She said she was scared and thought more than a few times about the wildlife and whether her dream was insane. Then she heard about the sixty-four-year-old woman who swam from Cuba to the United States and finally succeeded on her fifth try. At that point, she realized she was more afraid of the failure than the Atlantic, the jellyfish, or the whales.

Be the seventy-five-year-old getting her first university degree or the fifty-five-year-old who changes a child's life by becoming a teacher or volunteer. Don't quit on yourself at fifty—you are only halfway there.

I know this all sounds great, but you are probably thinking, *How do I get there?* It is one thing to want it and another thing to be able to afford it—whatever the *it* is. In this book, I have laid out thirteen lessons that I hope will assist you in reaching the *it*, your goals—whether they include owning a thirty-foot trailer or enjoying a happy, peaceful, fulfilling retirement or a break in the middle. I will help you move to an unconventional way of thinking when it comes to life and your money and one that I hope will provide you with great peace of mind and a plan for your future.

Most people believe they can't afford to change, and they are correct. Unless you step back, open your mind, and look at your finances in a different light, you won't be able to make a change. Paying yourself works; having goals and targets work; and spending time to truly understand how to get where you want to go *works*. Not saving or having a retirement plan, leaving your investments with an advisor, and not understanding what you have and how to grow these funds *does not work*.

My hope, in writing this book, is that you become encouraged and empowered to redefine yourself at every step of your life's journey, whether this be at young adulthood, midlife crisis, or retirement.

Every new beginning comes from some other beginnings end.—Seneca

LESSON 2:

HOW TO BEGIN: THE PLAN

A good plan violently executed today is better than a perfect plan executed next week. — George S. Patton

Our first adventure was in the thirty-foot trailer, but it wasn't just because I retired. That summer my oldest son, Brandon, was off to college in the States, and the next oldest, my seventeen-year-old daughter Heather, was on a yearlong class trip navigating the Pacific Ocean. It was an understatement to say we were a little jealous. We still had three kids at home, and of those, the oldest was only in first grade, so we set a goal. If we could rent out our house, we would travel. It worked. While the packing and planning were stressful, somehow it all got done, and we hit the road.

You can't buy a fridge, a boat, a house, or even a trailer to travel around North America without doing your homework first. Well, you can, but the more work you put into anything beforehand, the better the results you'll have. Our plan involved a budget, a time line, a trailer that could sleep five and a vehicle that could tow it, and some research about where to go.

How do you learn any trade, profession, accomplish any task, or learn a new skill unless you have a goal in mind? You can't even drive somewhere unless you know where you are going, how long it takes, and have directions. The same should be said about your finances and your future.

When you bring your car to a mechanic, you don't just drop it off at the door and walk away. You talk with the mechanic, explain the problem and what you want done—*the goal*. Then you get an idea of cost and timing before you go ahead with the work—*the plan*. If you were to come back and receive a bill four times more than the quote, get billed for items that were not discussed, or if your car still didn't work, you would be upset, and you wouldn't return to that garage.

It should be the same with your finances, and yet they are so much more important.

Over the years, many friends have asked if I could look over their portfolios. When I ask what they have in there, the answer is usually, "I don't know, that's why I pay my advisor."

This is true; you may have an advisor to help look after your investments or pension funds. What you may not know is where your money is being invested, the real cost to invest it, the performance of the fund, and how those investments align with your goals.

According to an ING Direct survey, Canadians spend an average of 3.4 hours per year planning their investments, whereas they spend 5 hours buying a smartphone, 6 hours planning a vacation, and 9.2 hours on a car purchase. Think about it—where does it make the most sense to spend your time?

A good advisor will help you complete a comprehensive discovery process, which is needed to assess your future direction and allows not only the advisor to see and evaluate the most reasonable way to accomplish your goals, but it also allows you to have a new view on where you are today and implement a concrete plan to move forward. Before this happens, though, you need to have a clear picture of where you want to be and when you want to get there. This is not only concerning your finances, but, more important, where you want to go in life and what is important to you. This allows you to connect your finances to your goals.

Remember, wishes are just desires, but dreams are goals that you have a fire in your belly to achieve.

Here are some questions you need to ask yourself:

- Where am I now?
- What motivates or drives me?
- What makes me happy?
- Where do I want to be in one, five, ten, and twenty years?
- Will I need an education fund? If so, how much will I need?
- How do I fund my retirement?
- When do I want to retire?
- How much do I need to live on now?
- How much do I need to live on after retirement?
- Do I want to leave a legacy after I'm gone?
- What is important to me?

Without answering questions like these and then assigning goals and targets to your answers, you will undoubtedly miss your goals, and yet this is so important. It is the path to your future.

Goals must have two things to be accomplished:

1. A concrete target date
2. A concrete dollar amount

If you plan to retire at sixty and hope to live to ninety and you would like to have $30,000 per year during those years, you now have a goal and can map out a plan.

Your goal is to have the present value of $30,000 in x years (by the time you are sixty) times thirty years in the future. Now you have a target, and you can create a strategy to get there.

Most people look at that figure and think there is no way—*I can't put aside that amount of extra cash every year.* So they ignore the problem and figure somehow it will work itself out. I can't think of a more important, life-altering issue to solve, and you don't need to save the full amount each year to reach your goal. There are opportunities to invest your money so that it's working to reach your long-term goals. The idea is not to ignore the challenge because you don't know how to get there; the idea is to state your goals and then get help to develop a realistic plan.

A partner of mine, who went from being worth more than $20 million to bankruptcy three times, said, "Steve, it is so easy to earn money, but so hard to hold on to it."

He is right. We have not been taught how to hold on to our money, regardless of how much we make. We really need to understand how a budget works, how to save, how to insure our assets, how to set financial goals and targets, and how to read a financial statement.

THE DISCONNECT

People are working hard, and some are saving blindly for the future. The problem is that they are not connected to their savings. Once you take the money from your paycheck and save it, you need a target, and you need to spend time and effort to create benchmarks for reaching those targets.

We had a corporation, family trust, registered retirement saving plan (RRSP), and a registered education savings plan (RESP), to mention a few. If there was a tax shelter or financial opportunity, we were there. By allocating funds properly, you will create more wealth by lowering or eliminating your taxes today or on the growth of those funds in the future. Through income sharing with your children or spouse, you can minimize your tax presence and spread the wealth. A good advisor accompanied by a good accountant can be great assets; but like everything in life, you must chose them wisely and understand their recommendations.

It is also very important to look at the whole picture. In our first big investment, our house, we made many construction errors, and some cost us dearly. We learned the hard way it was better to have a qualified person complete the work than have them fix your mistakes and then do the work. On one occasion, we thought we were being smart by hiring a contractor to install a new patio door. They wanted to purchase the door and have it ready on the day of their arrival. We wanted to save some money, so we purchased the door secondhand and picked it up ourselves on the night of the demolition. Of course, when we got it home in time for the installation, we discovered it was the wrong type of door. Now we had a hole in the side of our house and had not budgeted for the time or the cost of a new door. So the crew returned the next day to reinstall the old door.

I'm not saying that mistakes won't happen if we plan and make conscious decisions, but I am saying that we need to look at the whole project from start to finish before we begin, and the most important place to do this is with our investments and our portfolio.

You will be wealthier, mentally healthier, and have peace of mind about the future you have created...simply by setting your goals and saving for those goals *now*.

If you don't design your own life plan, chances are you'll fall into someone else's plan. And guess what they have planned for you? Not much. —Jim Rohn

LESSON 3:

HOW MONEY WORKS

It's not having what you want, it's wanting what you have.—Sheryl Crow

It's 2:00 a.m. in the winter 1992. I'm carrying my exhausted wife, who fell asleep on the floor, down a steep set of stairs in our first renovation house. It is dusty, dirty, dark, and I need to avoid the nails sticking out. Lord help me to get back to our apartment and sleep. At 6:00 a.m., our alarm will go off, and it will be time to get to our real jobs. Renovations can be stressful. We worked nights and weekends to make a complete disaster of a house into a beautiful home. We bought a run-down house in a great up-and-coming neighborhood, put in hours of sweaty labor, and it all paid off. This house gave us the start we needed to be on our way.

When I met Lisa, I was borrowing to pay my $3,500 monthly mortgage on my beautiful suburban home. My bills were higher than my income, and I needed to make a change. By selling my house, paying off my debt, and using the remaining $10,000 for a down payment on a less expensive house, we were able to start fresh. OK, so fresh meant an ugly, run-down house.

The next year's housing prices were down significantly, but because of the many hours of self-renovation and even mistakes, that house still increased in value.

MORTGAGES

We purchased the house for $179,000 with a $10,000 deposit, added $20,000 in renovation costs, and sold it two years later for $238,000.

~$179,000 – $10,000 + $20,000 = $189,000
~$238,000 –$158,000 (balance of mortgage)=$80,000
~$80,000 – ($39,755.60 mortgage payments)-$7,140 (real estate fees)=$33,104.40

By using leverage (the bank's money) as well as our sweat equity, we were able to make $33,104.40 or 110 percent on our $30,000 investment. Now we had a net worth of over $60,000 thanks to our savings and investment accounts. Three years before, we'd had no savings. We were able to succeed in a compromised real estate market. What a great start. It wasn't all easy. We had to be disciplined and have a budget. I am a spender, and of course I worked in an environment where people go through money like water. There were times when I would have to buy the entire trading desk lunch, so we had to budget for that kind of splurge. I also spent more time getting my shoes resoled than buying new ones; and, yes, a couple of times that meant hiding them under the desk because they had holes in the soles. Buying new $200 shoes was not an option. I think growing up a minister's son made clothes, gadgets, and expensive cars seem unnecessary.

We couldn't make the down payment work with only the $10,000, and the house was such a wreck that we were turned down for a standard Canadian mortgage and housing loan. So we had to go through a private lender arranged by our Realtor. That meant a second mortgage at a whopping 18 percent for another $14,000. Then we borrowed $3,000 each on a line of credit using our cars as collateral. We also had to max out our credit cards for renovations, but we knew it would take only four months to complete the renovations, and then we would be able to renegotiate the mortgage at a much better rate and pay off the second mortgage.

~Original value of the house: $179,000
~Down payment: $10,000
~First mortgage, 8 percent $1,137.19/month
~Second mortgage, 18 percent: $205.29/month
~Line of credit (cars),7 percent: $118.52/month
~Payment Total: $1,461/month
Four months later...
~New bank appraised value of
   the house: $230,000
~Value of our equity in the house: $63,000
~New bank-owned mortgage: $176,000
                                    at 7.25 percent
~New mortgage payment: $1,260.02/month

By increasing the equity or value in our home, we could then go with a traditional bank mortgage, amalgamating the first and second mortgages, credit card debt, and the car loans, to get a lower interest rate. This amalgamation saved us thousands of dollars in payments. Moreover, with our new equity we now had a much better bank profile, making us a much better client.

What do you do with the difference between the old mortgage payment and the new lower one? You have already adjusted your lifestyle to fit this payment, so don't buy a new TV, car, or clothes; stay at that payment rate, but use that difference to go directly into an investment account or pay down debt. In other words, the $200 a month we saved from renegotiating our loans could now be deposited into an investment account for our future. This way, you are not only thinking of your future, but you are also working on it and not on your current whims. There will be a pocket for that later. By the way, this is where most people fail. Every time they renegotiate their mortgage or get a bit of financial breathing room, they suck all the air out of the room with more spending and sacrifice their future for their immediate gain.

While my wife stayed focused on allocating certain dollars to certain financial obligations and goals, I ensured we stayed on target with our time lines so that the house was ready for remortgaging. We both believe paying yourself first is the key to success and avoiding burnout. So even on a tight budget, we allocated funds to our future, which meant a savings account, our RRSPs, and date night. Sometimes the last fund would have very little, but there was always enough to take a break and go for a stroll in our new neighborhood, returning to enjoy the fruits of our labor or to labor further.

Within three years we had a buyer for our house and were able to trade up to a better part of the city. We used the equity from the first house along with a new mortgage at a better rate and purchased a second house that also needed work. This time we required professional help, but to save money we did the general contracting, which was less manual labor for us but hours of phone calls and meetings. We purchased the home for $405,000 and put in $60,000 for renovations. After three years, we sold it for $585,000, a 25-percent return, less interest and real estate fees. After fees, it worked out to about 22 percent. We now had profits of $153,500 in real estate, whereas three years earlier we had $33,000, and six years earlier we had zero. Along with our RRSPs, other savings, and investment returns, our nest egg was growing fast.

In our continued search for houses with renovation potential, we were able to purchase at a low price, add value, and increase our net worth. We did not count on the real estate market to take the property value higher; we increased the homes' worth through sweat equity. If the market also went up, that was a bonus. Real estate is easy to research and understand; financing for it is readily available; the gains are not taxable if it is your primary residence; and you can choose how much of the work you are prepared to do and therefore how much of the return you will gain.

The real estate property exchange is much like any market, stock, or fund. Both you and the seller win! The seller values the money you paid them more than the property, and you value the property more than the money.

THE EXCHANGE

When we borrowed at 18 percent for a second mortgage on the first property, who won—the private lender or us?

We both won! They valued the chance of getting 18 percent more than the risk of our not paying. We valued the opportunity that the money gave us more than the high interest we would be paying.

A major misconception is that in any trade there is a winner and a loser. In his book, *Economics Made Simple*, Madsen Pirie states, "Trade is thus a win-win situation of benefit to both sides. Something else is true as well: an exchange makes both parties richer. After the trade each party has something more valuable than they had before."1

This can be in goods, stocks, mutual funds, currency, time, vacations, movies, or even dinners out. Therefore, any exchange creates wealth. Pirie goes on to say that "Some people are concerned to study and to understand what causes poverty, but even the question is a misconception. There are no causes of poverty – it is simply the absence of wealth. Poverty is the default condition: it is what happens when you do nothing."2

There is an interesting story about a group of kids from Paraguay who grew up in a landfill outside of the city center. Their lives were filled with drugs and gangs, until one of the garbage pickers, "Cola," who was known locally as a genius of the slums, got together with local musician Favio Chávez to make instruments for the children who lived in the dump. There was no money for real instruments, so together they started to make instruments from trash—violins and cellos from oil drums, flutes from water pipes, and spoons and guitars from packing crates. The kids taught themselves to play and started the "Landfillharmonic" and are now traveling around the world with these crude instruments, making incredible music and raising money for their plight. They didn't default; they did something to create wealth.

INFLATION AND INTEREST RATES

Inflation is having too much money chasing goods. When there is growth in the economy, people spend more. There is excess demand, therefore prices go up; this is called inflation. When you invest in anything or save, you have to earn more than the rate of inflation or you will have less buying power than when you began. If you put a $100 in the bank at 5 percent and inflation is 10 percent, the food you could have bought for $100 will now cost $110, but you will only have $105. Therefore, you will have to do with less food than you would have a year ago. This may not seem like an important point today, but it is essential as you plan for your retirement years. Therefore, you must always ensure that the return on your investments surpasses the rate of inflation today and in the future.

Gold, silver, and real estate are viewed as good hedges against inflation. They tend to increase in value over time, more than the prices of goods and services. I prefer real estate because you have some control and the ability to improve its value as well as earn rental income.

The average inflation rate over the last hundred years was about 3.2 percent, which is measured by the Consumer Price Index (CPI). Each month, the cost of a basket of goods is compared to the cost of those goods the previous month. If in retirement inflation rises, it means your money will not buy as many goods as it had before. The United States and Canadian governments aim to have steady 1–3 percent inflation. If inflation is low (as it is today), then they will lower interest rates to encourage spending and try to help prices rise. If inflation then begins to move at too high of a pace, the government will raise interest rates to discourage borrowing and spending in hopes of stabilizing inflation. In the 1970s inflation rates continued to rise at unprecedented rates, so the government continued to raise rates to the highest levels ever (16 percent). This worked and slowed the economy and inflation.

Most people accept inflation as a fact of life, and inflation is good, to a certain degree. It means prices are rising, incomes are rising, and the economy is rising, which is what we want, growth. However, for a retiree who is not earning but only spending dollars, inflation can be devastating, unless he or she is prepared and invested properly (we will discuss this in following lessons).

DEFLATION

While inflation is too much money chasing goods, deflation is too little money chasing goods. When the CPI falls, we call it deflation, meaning prices are decreasing—no growth. Since the American Civil War in the early 1860s, there has been only one extended period in North American history when overall prices decreased. It was after the crash of 1929, and it lasted for three years. Most of us weren't around during this phenomenon, nor do we believe it could ever happen; however, history shows that it can, and does, happen. In fact I believe we will be in a deflationary period in the very near future for years to come. We have more of a world economy today than we did back then, by which I mean that price changes are felt in every continent. For example, the price of oil is dependent on the demands of factories in China, and thus affects North American prices.

Deflation comes along at the end of a super-cycle or growth period. Since the late 1930s, we have been in a long-term eighty-year cycle: with growth during the 1940s–1950s, a slowdown or consolidation over the 1960s and 1970s, followed by massive growth in the 1980s and 1990s. We are close to the end of this long-term cycle. Lesson 9 will describe this type of spending cycle. When the supply/demand curve turns negative and there are more goods than buyers, or less money chasing goods, prices fall. Interest rates stay abnormally low, even with federal support. During these times real estate, oil, gas, food, and clothing could devalue against the dollar. If we look at the overall economic conditions and demographics, we can see that Japan is there, Europe is close, and North America is on their heels.

Deflationary periods are difficult. You may think that prices dropping is a win for consumers—cheaper cars, cheaper gas, cheaper groceries—but it also means negative returns on mutual funds, a reduction on stock prices and a drop in housing prices, and high unemployment, all the while things like mortgages stay the same. It is a time of negative growth, but there are opportunities if you are prepared. Think of this cycle as a life cycle, a season cycle, there is a spring (starting to see growth), a summer (a little breather and time to perfect), a fall (a time of rapid growth and euphoria), and a winter (a time to buckle down and reevaluate and get ready for the spring). Assets will be cheaper, which means a good time to build for the future. It is essential to look beyond the standard investment and savings vehicles and examine the opportunities and ultimately avoid risk.

EXCESS

When the housing market was skyrocketing in Florida, California, and Arizona it seemed like everyone, including our neighbor, had income property. One night, I had a long talk with that neighbor to try to convince him to be careful and sell some of his more than sixty residential holdings. He thought I was crazy and missing out on the *guaranteed* easy money that was to be made. He couldn't see the risk.

He was right. I had missed the euphoric upswing, but I also missed the downswing and the ultimate housing crash that followed.

When the time came and there were more sellers than buyers, prices plummeted. For my neighbor, that meant there were no buyers for his holdings, but he was still responsible for the taxes and mortgages on those sixty-plus properties. Eventually, he had to sell his beautiful retirement home and move into one of those properties. He gambled and lost!

Bad investors try to make money; good investors try not to lose money. Step one is concentrating on risk first, then the second step is looking at the potential gains.

The purpose of investing today is to forecast tomorrow's prices. You need to know when fear and greed will take over the fundamentals, and then when it will reverse.

By the time you hear it on CNBC, in the paper, or from your hairdresser, the game has changed. In 2008, the CEO of Wachovia, the fourth-largest bank in the United States stated on CNBC that the company was on a sound footing. Cramer on CNBC was then recommending the stock. Only three months later, they announce a $24 billion loss, which of course caused the stock to go down by a whopping 87 percent over the next four years.

You shouldn't always believe what management and CNBC are touting. Management is biased, and CNBC is listening to management.

A seasoned investor is happy to sell his or her holdings when everyone is getting in and then buy them back when there is panic and selling. "Dumb" money believes what it hears; "smart" money thinks for itself based on research and history.

Let's take the example of my neighbor again. He was buying the product (an unfinished condo) at $80,000 and selling it (finished) within a year for $180,000. It was an easy game, as long as there were buyers and he could sell his holdings, the condos, before taxes and mortgages were due. The game lasted for a few years, and he did very well. The problem was that he overextended his involvement and stayed in the game too long, even when the market indicators showed it was time to get out. Eventually, when the market tanked and there wasn't a bid for his properties, he had to walk away from his investments or sell them as a package for well below his purchase price. Buying low and then selling high sounds easy, but it's very difficult to implement unless you remove your emotions of fear and greed and look at these investments objectively. Stand back. Is the asset depressed? If so, it might be a buy. Is the asset inflated? If so, it might be a sell. Unfortunately most people do the opposite. When the price goes up, they tend to think it will go up forever and never want to sell; but when the price goes down, they are afraid and just want to get rid of it.

CANADIAN PENSION PLAN AND DEBT

In the late 1990s, the Canadian Pension Plan (CPP) began investing in equity holdings, and this resulted in Canadians having their pension funds vulnerable to the stock market and the proficiency of its managers. CPP and other private pension plans have run into major difficulties in the past thirteen years. The stock market has had two of the biggest corrections in history. The result of these corrections is that pension plans are left with far less than they forecasted. Exacerbating this fact is that when these plans were established, the workforce was filled with a population of baby boomers. Now those boomers are retiring, and the funds don't have the same influx of cash that they once experienced. Looking at our population numbers, we see a large number of people are in retirement stage, and there are not enough workers to keep the plans running as intended. I'll discuss this further in Lesson 9.

Compounding this problem, our life expectancy has greatly increased, so we are living longer and need those plans longer.

Suffice to say, we can't count on the government or even the private sector plans for retirement. We must be self-sufficient and plan for our own future. Our retirement is too important to count on the promises of politicians and pension fund advisers. And let's face it, they do not have the same interest in our retirement as we do.

On the other side of the border, things are not much better. The US government has been printing $118 million an hour or $85 billion a month for the last five years through their quantitative easing process to shore up the economy and create growth. The $14 trillion deficit is only part of the truth. Off-balance sheet obligations such as Treasury debt issued, Medicare, and Social Security reportedly put the true debt at between $60–$80 trillion, which amounts to $170,000 per person or $665,000 per family. At some point we all have to pay our bills.

According to Peter Schiff, CEO, Euro Pacific Capital, "The Fed knows that the US economy is not recovering...it simply is being kept from collapse by artificially low interest rates and quantitative easing. As that support goes, the economy will implode."3

As of November 2014, that support has ended.

Whether that happens in entirety or not, it is important to see the risks and to plan accordingly so that you are not there to be blindly run over.

IT'S YOUR MONEY

So how do you avoid the risk? It's simple: don't depend on others. Understand what you have.

Neither Americans nor Canadians should count on the government funding their retirement. If some funding is available, great, but we shouldn't bet our future on it.

You also can't give your money to an advisor and walk away. You need to know where your money is, what you own, and why. You also need retirement goals and targets. You work hard for your money; you want to enjoy retirement. Let the money you worked so hard to earn work for you now. Understanding, planning, and action are the *only* ways to ensure your goals.

Recently, I had the misfortune of being out on my boat when the engine started smoking. It was my first sail after the winter, so when I saw white smoke coming from the engine exhaust, I assumed it was just burn-off.

We weren't going far, so we just put up the sails, turned off the engine, and ignored the problem. That was my first mistake.

When we rounded the corner an hour later and cranked the engine to set the anchor, there was not only smoke from the exhaust, but it was also pouring out of the engine room.

We quickly put down our hook, and thankfully it held even in the middle of the channel. We were also thankful to have a no-wind forecast. After a restless night of thinking, I realized the seacock was closed, and there was no water to cool my engine. The damage was done. I was lucky enough to reach my mechanic and have him come out and fix the consequences of my mistake, but I got a well-deserved earful.

When I told my mechanic that I've never closed the seacocks, he told me that I should have checked.

He reminded me that I now needed to have my engine flushed, and he suggested that I take some notes. I asked if I could just count on him doing it when he had a chance, and I got another earful. That was my second mistake.

"Who knows where I will be?" he replied. "You need to take care of your boat. You paid a lot of money for this, and you need to be in charge to ensure work is done. You can't depend on others to do it for you."

What a wake-up call. It was exactly what I had been preaching to people about their money. The boat was the same. When Pete talked poly-whatever or Racor versus Volvo filters, I stopped listening. But each time I zoned out, it was costing me thousands of dollars in unnecessary repairs. I needed to stop disconnecting, so I could understand and monitor my investment. I needed to learn how to take care of what I had worked so hard to have and not simply depend on the so-called experts to care for it for me.

I needed to educate myself on what I should be doing on a regular basis to check on my investment. I needed to ensure the maintenance I requested was getting done and that there was no miscommunication. I needed to have a list with regular checks for myself to ensure I didn't get into trouble with the boat or at least avoid the common pitfalls.

And it is the same with your money.

You should start your list by breaking down your income: separate what you bring in and what you pay out. Look at your must-pays, like your mortgage/rent and loans and then your spending habits. Then look at your investments and savings. You need to know what is going out, where it is going, and what it is making. Pete was willing to talk with me to develop that list; you need an adviser who will do the same. He was willing to take the time and help me understand the investment I had and how it worked, using terms and re-describing mechanical workings until I could grasp their purpose. You need an adviser who will do the same so that you don't zone out.

If you have already answered your questions, listed your goals, and created your targets, now you need to start saving and understanding where those savings are going or where they can go. There are many forms of investments.

Blessed are the young for they shall inherit the national debt.—Herbert Hoover

Lesson 4:

SAVING—THE ONLY WAY TO CREATE WEALTH

Beware of little expenses. A small leak will sink a great ship.—Benjamin Franklin

The only way to create wealth is to save it when you make it. Period.

You can save in a bank account, pay off debt (so you are saving in interest), or invest in something you understand. The bottom line is that you need to be saving when you are making. By paying yourself early and first, you have a greater chance of greater return.

By putting away $1,000 today and adding $200 monthly at 2 percent, which is the current bank rate, you will have the following:

~$5,942.00 in two years
~$27,809.37 in ten years
~$79,541.87 in twenty-five years

Money grows exponentially as time goes by, but we can't forget that inflation is also currently 2 percent. That doesn't mean we should forget about savings; it means we need to look at other vehicles. This way you will have a nest egg by simply putting a little aside to pay yourself.

Saving is not just what you take off the top of your paycheck and put away. Saving is the mutual or pension fund you have invested in at work; it's the RESP you have for your children's education fund; it's the mortgage that you pay off every month; it's the insurance that you pay into. Savings are all those puddles of money that leave your income but do not disappear on consumed products like electronics and gadgets.

Unfortunately, most of the time, there doesn't seem to be enough money to go around, let alone to put something aside. Most live paycheck to paycheck. But I like to look at savings as our food for the future. If we don't put it away today, we may be hungry tomorrow. Just like that mortgage and tax payment, or the car and house insurance that went up, somehow we find a way to make it work. Savings should be the same—the payment that we know has to come out of our paycheck. I finally learned this lesson when I downsized to that first ugly house and had a mortgage that I could afford, which meant that I had a savings plan that I could also afford.

The recommended savings is 10 percent of your pay, but it is far better to supplement these savings with real estate projects or financially lucrative hobbies that will help you reach your target. We just need to set a realistic goal of saving a certain amount in a specific time, and then we need a plan for it.

Saving, planning, and working today doesn't mean we are not or cannot enjoy today. On the contrary, I believe that these goals help us have more fun. It may mean that those new shoes may have to be the cheaper ones, the dinner out may be ice cream this week, and the movie may have to be on cheap night. Again, the important part is not to stop living; it is making choices so that you reach your goals. Now when you do something to reward yourself, it will mean so much more because it is the prize you have worked for and therefore it will give you greater pleasure. You also have the comfort of knowing you haven't sacrificed your future along the way.

In saving your money, it is important to first look at where your disposable income is going. I have a sister-in-law who, in her words, was addicted to the store Winners. There was a store close to her house, and once a week, she would go over for a visit before work. She said all those great deals were killing her. Rather, they were killing her finances. So in her new plan she set a budget for her visits and went every two weeks instead. She even rewarded herself on the alternative weeks with a much more economical visit to the bead store, where she was buying goods she was using for creating and selling, which would actually make her money.

By changing her habit, she was able to save $600 a month. Here is how. Currently, she was spending $200 a visit, which she said was her average. This was a whopping $800 a month or the cost of half her mortgage. When she cut it back to $100 a visit and went every second week, she was halving her spending and her visits, so she was down to $200 a month versus $200 a week. At first she thought it would be hard, but in the end she was putting her new prized possessions on layaway and feeling great about the retirement fund she had been ignoring all those years.

The second part of savings is to ensure that your goals are aligned with your life and hobbies. The first summer my wife and I were together, we spent every available free weekend and drove four hours to my uncle's farm to work on a wooden boat he had given us. We sanded and toiled and purchased everything from new sails at $2,000, a used trailer for $700, and a motor for $1,200 to name a few. In the end we had spent over $5,000 and countless hours on a boat that didn't even work for our family, all for the lure of something free. The only thing we increased was our debt. After our first sail, we were wise to our mistake and frustrated with our lack of vision. We put the boat up for sale and were thankful that we recouped $1,000 of our investment. The little wooden boat was our first lesson in alignment; our hobby/passion didn't align with our financial goals.

If you are spending money on a project, make sure it is going to reap you a financial reward in the end. The boat would not reward us at the time of sale, so we were spending our retirement. It is also important not to be a slave to your investments or hobbies. One summer, my son Brandon was watching me gardening yet again. While I love gardening, he pointed out that he hadn't seen me sit and enjoy the garden, the pool, or the beach. He was so right. Even though everything was looking perfect, I was not living perfect. I needed to enjoy more.

My in-laws also reminded me again of the importance of alignment. In summer 2000, I secured for them, in my words, "a no-fail investment." I knew the investment manager, loved his philosophy, and could see that his fund had nowhere to go but up. My in-laws left their investment with him for the year and watched it go up and down, but in the end, even though they were up on their investments, they decided they would much rather have a cottage with their savings.

They bought a great piece of real estate that needed a ton of work and slowly renovated it from top to bottom. Their first priority was safety, so they rewired it. Their second priority was fun, so they built a huge dock and bought a number of water toys. All the while, I thought they were crazy. They were using their retirement savings to have fun. But they slowly picked away at the improvements, spending their disposable income, and ten years later they had dramatically increased their original investment.

The money they had been spending at Home Depot was better than what I spent at West Marine; it was rewarding them with their financial future and allowing them to move forward with their retirement. They had enjoyed their investment with the kids all those years, and now that they were in college they were cashing in and buying that retirement place in Florida. They knew they needed a project, but rather than one that racked up a debt, they chose one that would help with their future goals and meet their current needs.

Their passions and hobbies aligned with their goals.

The trick is to ensure that your hobbies don't run you credit card poor. Credit cards are only to be used for purchases that you can pay for at the end of the month. They should never be seen as a line of credit; you need to ensure that what you spend can be afforded and paid at the end of every month. The credit-monitoring agency TransUnion predicts that the average Canadian consumer's total non-mortgage debt will have hit an all-time high of $28,853 by the end of 2014. It is imperative that we examine that debt and understand its potential impact on our future.

The person who earns $200,000 a year may appear wealthier than the person who earns $40,000 a year, yet their savings and future may be very different. Let's say the higher earner spends and consumes goods like cars and clothes, which are depreciating assets. And the higher earner goes out on a weekly basis for an expensive dinner—in other words, spending everything and saving nothing. Now, the lower earner saves 10 percent of his or her income. Over time, the person with the higher income consumed all his or her earnings and has nothing to show for his or her hard work. Alternatively, the person with the lower income has saved and accumulated compound interest and returns, which will be used in the future.

Discipline and alignment are needed to create wealth. Here is a test formula for expected net worth:

~Wealth should be = present age x pretax income (total life earnings)/10

If your number is lower than it need be, it should be a wake-up call for change.

When we purchased our first house, it was apparent that we needed a strict budget. OK, so my wife said we needed a budget, and she was right. Snip went the credit cards, and out came the envelopes. Every two weeks, on payday, we would go to the bank, deposit our checks, pay

our mortgage, pay our 10 percent for savings and investments, and the rest would come home and go in envelopes. There was an envelope with cash for each bill, and
then an envelope for groceries, gas and transportation,
lunch money, dinners out, and vacation. If our bills were
higher than we had budgeted, we would take from the
dinner or lunch envelope and pack a lunch and eat dinner at home. We would still go out, except it would be
for ice cream or a glass of wine rather than a full dinner. Most times, however, now that we were watching
our spending, we were coming in under budget, so we
had an overflow envelope for emergencies and extras
and an investment top-up plan. While those envelopes
were a pain, by seeing the amount of cash it was costing to run our house, we were much more inclined to put
on a sweater and slippers and turn down the heat. We
were also buying soup sometimes for lunch rather than a
sandwich. During that time, we never went without, and
we felt more in control of our money. Those date nights
and vacations were sweet—we earned them—and the
hard work, conversation, and planning became an inte-
gral part of our relationship foundation.

It is important to understand the real meaning of assets and liabilities. An asset is something that either creates a gain or creates cash flow. A liability is something

that costs you money. Some say your house is a liability, because you are continuing to finance it. Technically, this is true, especially during 2008,2009 in the United States. The stock market was down, housing prices were plummeting, and insurance costs were going up. So there was no cash flow, no gains—just money out of pocket and a depleting asset, in other words, a liability.

Many walked away from their houses because what they owed on their mortgages was more than what their houses were worth. Families who had spent years paying their mortgages were now paying rent with no asset and were financially ruined.

Some people took a different approach. With so many without a home, the rental industry took off. One friend moved his family out of their home and rented it out for more than the cost of the mortgage. With that headache taken care of, he was able to rent a smaller home, at a cost substantially lower than his mortgage. This meant he had eliminated a huge portion of his monthly costs but still had his investment for the future.

Another friend used his vacation home in Utah. When insurance rates went sky high, the family really felt the pinch. Rather than downsizing and selling the property, where they vacationed only two to four weeks a year, they turned it into a short-term rental property.

By making a few changes, like putting locks on the closets, putting away their personal items, changing to rental insurance, and hiring a property manager, they were able to rent their property for weekly stays and have others pay the mortgage.

In both cases, these friends used their "liabilities" and turned them into assets, which meant the vacation property that was once costing them on a monthly basis was now making them money. Their first goal was to have the property stop costing them, but in the end it became a good investment. These examples happened during a tough market, so they saved more during the downturn than they did when times were good.

By being creative with your assets, you are letting them work for you, thus creating wealth even in times of financial crisis.

All the toys and gadgets, latest inventions, cars, newest designer clothes, and new state-of-the art phones are part of the consumption generation we have created. They rob us of our savings, our future, our peace of mind; they rob us from truly enjoying life. Sadly they also own us. We trade the future for the now.

Remember, a trade takes place when we give up something we value less in exchange for something we value more. Trade creates wealth, so be sure the wealth is on your side. Perspective and being conscious of your financial decisions, no matter how small, is key to holding on to your money.

> *Save a part of your income and begin*
> *now, for the man with a surplus controls*
> *circumstances and a man without surplus is*
> *controlled by circumstance.—Henry Buckley*

LESSON 5:

THE TRUTH ABOUT MUTUAL FUNDS

Insanity: doing the same thing over and over again and expecting different results.—Albert Einstein

Friends and acquaintances come up to me on a regular basis and ask, "What mutual fund should my money be in? I haven't done well with Mutual Fund A. Should I switch to Mutual Fund B?"

I'm not going to be specific with fund names here, because my point applies to the majority of funds.

When approached, my first question is always the same: "What type of fund are you in? An actively managed or a passive fund? A balanced equity or bond fund?"

Almost always, the response is, "I don't know. My advisor looks after that."

And when I ask what their investments are for, it's almost always, "This is for my retirement. Hopefully I'll get great returns, and then I can retire early."

It is easy to see that there are no expectations, just blind hope.

Before you can understand mutual funds, you need to understand the stock or equity market, which is simply an open market for individuals to come and buy or sell pieces of publicly owned companies in the form of stock—not socks, as my children once thought of them. Mutual funds are a basket of stocks; stocks are pieces of companies; companies are people making money. The market is comprised of many companies that are put into sectors, for example the oil and gas sector would have companies like Petro-Canada and Shell Canada.

Within the market there are a number of different indexes, which are comprised of a group of stocks. One of the oldest is the Dow Jones Industrial Average (DJIA), which includes thirty of the largest and most well-known companies in the United States. In Canada, there is the Standard & Poor/Toronto Securities Exchange (SPX/TSX). Again, this is simply a grouping of some of the largest and most well-known and respected corporations.

For now, let's look at mutual funds. When you buy into a mutual fund, Wall Street, Bay Street, the banks, the media, your adviser, and many friends will advise you to buy actively managed funds, and buy the ones that have done well over the last two to three years. There is a major flaw in this advice and continuing to work within this paradigm.

Actively managed mutual funds (AMFs) are funds invested and maintained by portfolio managers. Their job is to outperform the market indexes, but history proves they do not. For a variety of reasons, it is very difficult, if not impossible, for an AMF manager to have a rate of return that is greater than an index.

First, I would like to address why these products are offered. Brokers and their firms consistently make millions of dollars by having your money in their AMFs; they are paid through a management expense ratio (MER), which are management fees paid by you, regardless of your return. According to the *Financial Post*, between 1997 and 2013 AMFs under-performed the index by 89.7 percent in Canadian equities, 94.4 percent in US equities, and 88.9 percent in international equities.4

Yet, fund managers continue to persuade you or your advisor to "buy and hold" their AMFs and have you believe that their managers can outperform the market and you should pay higher fees for this expertise. According to Larry Swedroe on CBS *MoneyWatch*, "If you are a passive investor and you don't want to be involved with the market, you pay low fees. They [investment firms] don't want low fees...getting you to be passive takes money out of their pocket."5

In a later comment he also states, "As investors learn and get fed up with bad outcomes, they'll wake up to this. It will happen as sure as the ocean is eroding the shore."5

Imagine paying top dollar to get your roof fixed, only to have it leak worse the next time it rains. Yet, in the financial industry, getting paid for inferior work seems to be acceptable.

In the first part of 2014, an American friend of mine was very excited to share with me that after switching equity funds the previous year from company A equity fund to company B equity fund, his performance had greatly improved. Last year alone he was up a whopping 16.5 percent. He was ecstatic. I felt bad bursting his bubble, but knew he should understand. During the same period since he had switched, the S&P 500 Index was up just over 29 percent. He had under-performed the market by over 12.5 percent and had paid a fee of 2.5 percent to get that return. What had company A's performance been last year? He didn't know.

He could have switched to a passive index fund, which is also sold by most dealers for a smaller fee (usually less than 1 percent) and received roughly 28 percent return after fees. He also could have watched both funds on his computer screen or in the newspaper in order to follow their performance.

You need to know what you own and why you are in these specific funds. You should be watching your money on at least a quarterly basis and have clear expectations and targets to reach on a yearly or biyearly basis. If that isn't happening, you need to understand why and have options for change.

To understand why these actively managed funds are under-performing, you need to see inside the industry. For the most part, these managers' hands are tied, and there are a few reasons why these well-intending active managers are unable to outperform the market.

COSTS

The cost of an active management team is expensive. They need analysts, portfolio managers, office staff, and the cost of trading is higher. An active fund then needs to outperform the market just to break even. A passive style or index fund simply buys stocks in the index at the equivalent weight and doesn't require the higher expenses.

A mutual fund has expenses to run the fund, and these costs are passed on to you.

Management fee + operating expenses + taxes = MER

The cost of trading is extra and is also deducted from gains.

According to the Vanguard Investments, the average total MER costs are as follows:

	Actively Managed	Passive/ Index	ETFs (Equity Traded Funds)*
Canadian Equity	2.2%	.85%	.21%
Canadian Bonds	1.3%	.75%	.32%

* Equity Traded Funds will be explained later in the lesson.

TIME

By the time you have done your research and identified a good manager, the fund could be too large or even closed to new investors. A smaller fund has an easier chance of outperforming than a large one, because the bigger the fund, the longer it takes to decide and implement a position of change. It takes longer to buy or sell a large position or a large quantity of a stock. Because of their volume in the market, or the amount of a company's stock that they own, the managers actually move the stock in the opposite direction before they can complete the trade. For example, a large fund might try to sell holdings/shares in Bell Canada and use the proceeds to accumulate a new position in Petro-Canada to have more oil exposure in their portfolio. The problem is that because the fund has such a large holding in Bell, selling will draw attention. Brokers and clients see this activity as dumping the stock. They are left to wonder why they're selling and what the problem may be with Bell.

So the stock moves lower. The same is true, of course, on the other side, and as they try to buy Petro-Canada, it will creep up because of the increased demand. Thus these large funds with their large capital positions tend to move stock, but in the opposite direction than they had desired. They have a second option of buying or selling slowly over a long period, but this is not easy, and it takes months to accomplish, which may lead them to miss the opportunity at hand.

PERFORMANCE

Managers move around from one firm to another, which means the fund you own may not be managed by the same person that was there when you bought it. Each manager has a different style and reacts differently in a variety of trading situations.

It's like a good chef at a restaurant. The food we eat, like the money they trade, is based on the style of the person in charge.

When I first started covering Frank Mersch at Altamira in 1987, he had about $20 million in a newly formed mutual fund. It was a young company, promising great performance. With Frank at the helm, Altamira amassed over $7 billion in equities by 1998. By 2006, the picture was very different. Frank had left, and Altamira had lost almost half of its value and was down to $3.7 billion in assets. When different managers have different styles, different results occur. Even managers who try to follow the same set of goals and principles see investments differently, and therefore the results are never the same.

You see, Frank knew people and how to get them to work for him. In the first trade I did with him, he asked how much commission I would like to get paid. This was at a time when you would get $0.05 a share, so I said $0.06 would be amazing. He offered $0.10 (on a 1.2 million share order, this was $120,000 in commission in just one trade), but on the condition that he would be the first call on any trade. Of course, I'm sure he made the same deal with all the other traders on the street, and this became a big part of his successful career.

He was one of the first real contrarians in the Canadian market. Instead of beating brokers down on commissions, he overpaid, thereby getting the best and most important information first. Information is what makes markets move. The market is made up of humans, and consequently human negotiations play into its success. Frank knew that humans could make or break his success. If our analyst lowered a rating on a stock, Frank was our first call. If we were issuing stock and had a limited supply, Frank was our first call and always got the best fill.

MANDATE

Because fund managers invest for the long term and have a buy-and-hold mandate, even when they believe the whole stock market is expensive and that it will crash or head lower, their hands are tied. An equity fund's mandate is to invest; roughly 95 percent of their holdings in equities and a maximum of 5 percent are in cash. So when the market is at the top and the business cycle has run its course and peaked, the only option they have is to move their more aggressive positions to more defensive positions, or, in other words, watch their stocks and your money lose value.

This also means they cannot switch to bonds or cash, and they are mandated to have a certain amount of holdings in each market sector. They can't sell all of their oil stocks or technology stocks; they can only reduce their position by possibly 1 or 2 percent. Many times their only option is to wait and hope the market doesn't fall too much. Many of you may be reading and understanding this for the first time, but these rules and standards are developed by the industry. You would have had to sign off on the prospectus or state that you understood the mandate when you put your money into the fund.

What then should you invest in?

ALTERNATIVES TO ACTIVELY MANAGED MUTUAL FUNDS

Passively Managed Funds or Index Funds

In Canada, the S&P/TSX Composite Index is an index of the largest companies on the Toronto Stock Exchange. An indexed equity fund would mirror the TSX. They are not traded on a basis of feeling, but are held to perform the same as the market and are available from investment firms. Some other indexes include the S&P 500 (United States) and the Nikkei 225 (Japan).

The costs to the investor are usually less than half of an AMF, and performance is not an issue, as it performs to the benchmark and is not intended to outperform. Also, there are no emotions involved. If you want to be in the market and want the returns of the market, or close to it, a passively managed fund or index fund can be a better option than an AMF. That said, you still need to understand market timing and try to avoid unnecessary risk.

While these options are widely available through pension fund and mutual fund companies, there are other options that require an adviser or an individual brokerage account.

Hedge Funds

Another option to be exposed to the market is a hedge fund. The difference between a mutual fund and a hedge fund is quite simple. An actively managed fund has a mandate to outperform the index, while hedge funds have a mandate of pure performance. Therefore, hedge fund managers do not have to be concerned if the index or any market is up or down. They are only interested in the highest possible return, no matter what the markets are doing. While both mutual and hedge funds have experienced major losses at times and some have gone completely under, many hedge funds have also experienced huge returns. There is a cost for the opportunity to reap substantial returns, and you see this in its fee structure.

Hedge funds are generally viewed by regulators as being higher risk than mutual funds, because management is not governed by the same strict rules as mutual funds. Hedge funds usually charge a 1-2 percent management fee, which is in line with mutual funds, but they usually have a 10-20 percent performance fee as well. The manager will reap a percentage of the reward when the investor makes money. By charging this performance fee, the hedge fund manager and the investor are aligned. The hedge fund manager is now more motivated than his mutual fund competitor, because he will make much more money as you make much more money. During up and down markets, a hedge fund is also allowed a variety of trading techniques:

~They can cash in their stocks or positions and sit in cash.

~They can go long, which means they buy equities or stock with the belief that the stock will go up.

~They can go short, also referred to as shorting a stock, which in essence means they borrow the stock from a broker with the belief that the stock value is going down. This way, if Bell Canada is trading at $40 a share and they believe the market is correcting or that stock is going down in value, they can short the stock. When or if it goes down, they can cover their short by buying back the stock and make the difference between their sale price and their purchase price.

~They can also use derivatives, such as options and futures.

The important fact is that these fund managers and your investments have options during times of market fluctuation; their only mandate is to make money.

While hedge funds have been around for more than twenty-five years, governing bodies state they are available only to pension funds and accredited investors whose net worth is more than $1 million (not including primary residence) or whose income is higher than $200,000 (or $300,000 including spouse). One of the best returns I have ever had was with a hedge fund. As with all fund managers, we need to be careful when choosing a hedge fund manager. And remember, there is risk in any investment; past performance does not the future make.

Private Equity

There are also private equity funds that raise money for start-up or young growth companies, much like those on the TV shows *Dragon's Den* or *Shark Tank*. They pool together private money and decide which companies to support financially. Your money is now invested in young companies, but with the watchful eye of the fund manager. Performance is not public; therefore, it is difficult to evaluate. Almost all major financial institutions invest in a number of these firms, but it is usually through a personal contact. Most of these private equity funds are formed through a limited liability partnership (LLP). Again, you need to invest a minimum of $150,000, because they are not regulated like public equity and therefore are seen to be a higher risk.

Equity Traded Funds

An equity traded fund (ETF) is much like a mutual fund in that it also holds a basket of stocks. An ETF is traded on the stock exchange and therefore increases or decreases in value based on supply and demand. These funds were set up to mirror a particular sector, index, commodity, or other asset classes.

ETF advantages are as follows:

- There is one cost for one trade.
- It is simple to work with.
- There is no prospectus to fill out or sign.
- You can check the price at any moment.
- They are cost effective with lower management fees.
- You have flexibility with what you own in your portfolio.
- You can buy or short the market or a sector.
- You can change quickly from one asset class to another.
- They are transparent, so you can see what you have in your portfolio.
- Taxes are lower.

These benefits are very important. If you feel or if indicators suggest that oil is going up, you can have a strong presence in the oil sector or oil stocks in your portfolio immediately.

Tax implications are lower with ETFs, because they only create capital gains or losses. They are taxed at the lowest rate, as opposed to mutual funds, which pay higher taxes on dividends and income-paying assets.

Inverse Traded Funds

An inverse ETF is simply the inverse of how a sector or market performs. It goes up at roughly the same percentage as the market or sector goes down. If you feel oil is going down, you simply buy an inverse oil ETF, and, like magic, you are now shorting the oil sector and will benefit if you are correct and it does go down. If you believe your investments are going down but are unable to cash in, you can insure or hedge your positions with an inverse ETF (this will be covered further in Lesson 11).

INSURED ANNUITIES

An insured annuity is a life annuity and a life insurance product purchased together. The annuity provides a regular income stream, and the insurance provides a cash payout at death. The combination is ideal for individuals seeking guaranteed income and preservation of capital. The insured annuity pays a higher guaranteed after-tax income for life, compared to traditional interest-bearing low-risk products (such as Treasury bills [T-bills] and Guaranteed Investment Certificates [GICs]). Let me demonstrate:

FINANCIAL BENEFITS

GIC investment @ 3 percent	Monthly income (single life)	Insured annuity
$400,000	Total capital invested	$400,000
N/A	Single deposit life insurance payment	N/A
N/A	Life annuity premium	$400,000
$1,000	Cash flow	$2,480
$1,000	Taxable income	$200
$460	Taxes payable at 46 percent tax rate	$92
N/A	Ongoing insurance premium	$1,121
$540	Net income	$1,267
$400,000	Estate value	$400,000

A 7.04 percent Rate of return on a GIC would be needed to achieve the insured annuities after tax income. A rate that is unheard of today for a risk-free product (U.S. T-bills and Canadian GIC's are considered risk-free).

We have looked at a number of alternatives for where you should house your money. Whether you stay with your current Actively Managed Fund, switch to a Passive Fund, ETF'S, or evaluate other options for your investments, it is important to remember a few things.

The Truth about Mutual Funds

1. When you invest in mutual funds, you are invested in the stock market, because a mutual fund is simply a basket of stocks.
2. You pay a premium for an AMF, but historical data proves that they under-perform their benchmarks and are outperformed by passive (index) funds.
3. There are other options, like hedge and index funds, but like every investment, you need to monitor them, have performance benchmarks, and be aware of market timing and market cycles.

The shepherd always tries to persuade the sheep that their interest and his own are the same.—Stendhal

Lesson 6:

MARKET THEORIES—WHY BEING A CONTRARIAN WORKS

Whenever you find yourself on the side of the majority, it is time to pause and reflect.—Mark Twain.

A couple of years ago, I participated in a school experiment and a chance to teach my children about trading and the market: I held a competition. For four weeks, we each had $1 hundred thousand in virtual money to invest. My youngest son, Levi, who is notorious for thinking outside the box, won. Given that he was only ten at the time and unwilling to be bored by the fundamental research of stocks, I inquired about his success.

He was quite clear that he only looked at the charts, watched for visual movements in large capitalized stocks, and when he found one that was particularly strong and captured his interest, he read a few lines.

The CEO of one company was caught in an affair and in the middle of a messy divorce. In simple terms, Levi figured this couldn't be good for the company or the stock, so he shorted it, made a killing, and cashed in his virtual earnings, winning the competition. Levi reinforced how important it is to look outside the box and understand that you can follow emotion in trading without being emotional.

The next three lessons will give you detailed information on the market, how to understand why and when it fluctuates, and how you can react to these changes to minimize your risk.

If you find that the information is too technical and out of your area of interest, just scan the charts and move to Lesson 9. But remember, everyone can trade, or at least understand the market, even if you only understand basic human nature.

First, let's look at the development of the market and how some of the products we invest in today came to be. Theories are not always constant, nor are they always complete. Sometimes the easiest theories to understand

and comprehend are the ones that are given credence. Unfortunately, that does not mean the theory is correct : the world isn't flat.

Back in the 1960s, the financial industry made a decision to sell their financial products to the masses. Previously, the general public had little access, nor did they think they could afford, to be involved in the stock market. To do this, the industry would need to identify the risks of investing and to market their products; they would need to measure and justify these risks. It would be no easy task, but it was deemed necessary to sell products. The question was, which fund, bond, stock, index, or derivative would have the best risk/reward ratio?

The brokerage industry, the rating agencies, the advisors, and the clients needed to know which investments were risky and which were more risk averse, and they needed to offer potential clients concrete numbers as well as a rationalization to the managers who would sell their products.

Much hypothesizing, theory development, and modeling ensued, some of which held for the industry while some fell away. It is important to understand that while two main theories stuck, the regulatory bodies, and thus the investment industry, firmly believe in the first (Random Walk Theory).

1. THE RANDOM WALK THEORY

The Random Walk Theory states that past price on a stock or a market has no bearing on its future movement. Stock prices are random, and there is no way to predict whether they will move up or down. Of course, this theory does not bode well for an industry trying to sell a product based on predicting future prices, so the Efficient Market Hypothesis (EMH) was born within the Random Walk Theory.

Expanding on the Random Walk Theory, EMH states that at any point in time, securities reflect all available information, and that information is reflected in the stock, immediately. Therefore, it is impossible to predict the market or to outperform the market. With this belief, the industry needed some sort of risk model to be able to sell products, and the capital asset pricing model (CAPM) was developed.

The CAPM formula uses *beta*, which is simply a measurement of how much a stock moves versus the overall market or other asset, in other words, volatility. They continued to hypothesize that volatility is the same as risk, and that all information is in the stock. The bottom line for the investor to understand is that according to the theory, if a stock moves up or down *less* than the overall market, it is deemed a lower risk; if a stock moves up or down *more* than the market, it is deemed a higher risk. If bonds move up or down less than stocks, then they are deemed less risky (regardless of interest rates, even though they determine the movements of bonds).

So a beta of 1.7 means that a stock moves up or down on average 70 percent more than the general market; therefore, that stock is perceived as risky. Whereas a beta of .7 means that a stock will fluctuate within only 70 percent of the overall market; therefore, that stock is deemed less volatile or less risky than the overall market.

They now had the proof needed to sell or justify products to their clients. CAPM and EMH became, and still are, accepted gauges for the market, all asset classes, hedge funds, commodities, and even mutual fund volatility. Unfortunately, continued research has shown that there is absolutely no correlation to volatility and price movements over time.

In his book, *Contrarian Investment Strategies: The Psychological Edge,* David Dreman reveals that the evidence from many research articles concludes that high volatility does not give better results, nor does lower volatility give worse results. This means that the funds your advisor says are low risk really means low volatility, and low volatility has not been proven to equate with low risk.

2. INEFFICIENT MARKET THEORY

Another theory that was prevalent was the Inefficient Market Theory, which states that because of human influence, the way different investors evaluate information is *not* efficient. In other words, all investors do not act in the same manner, and therefore emotions and human behaviour cause stock prices and markets to be inefficient.

The contrarian point of view was then born, which states that you can profit from investing in a manner that differs from the conventional wisdom when the conventional wisdom appears to be wrong. Stocks do move in identifiable directions.

In reviewing, but more important working with these theories, I've learned that the only way to evaluate how much risk is in an asset or stock is to examine historical performance. A stock's frequent movement up or down does not determine risk. Price history is the only evidence we have to identify risk—not how much it moves, but the direction it moves.

Risk is the potential of losing something of value weighted against the potential to gain something of value. We make risk/reward decisions at every step of life, including our investments. When we have inflation, the money we save is at risk; during deflation, the risk is that our assets are losing value. Whether we are buying bonds or equities, or sitting in cash, we are always at risk. We need to understand which asset class has the best odds of increasing and the least risk of decreasing over a specific period. Investors must truly understand that when you invest in any asset, there *is* risk.

A baseball manager will put in a left-handed pitcher to face a left-handed batter in key times, because the odds of success are better. A hockey coach will put on his top-scoring line and pull the goalie in the final minute of a game when down a goal, because the odds of scoring are better. A police officer will call for backup when the odds of confrontation are greater. Insurance companies base their premiums on the odds of an event happening, and that's why young drivers have such high premiums. The odds or statistics state that they are a higher risk. Odds are simply the assumption of risk/reward, not a guarantee, but an educated statistical assumption. History is our only teacher, so we use it to develop the odds we are willing to take.

When we invest, the goal should not be, simply to find the best reward only; it should be to find the best risk adjusted reward that will help me reach my goals over my investment time. Bonds have risk if interest rates go up; cash has risk if inflation rises; and equities have risk if we have a slowdown in the economy. Interest rates tend to take many years to go up or down. Inflation rises and falls similar to interest rates in long-term trends. On the other hand, the stock market tends to go up 65 percent of the time in almost any two, five, ten, or twenty-year period. Knowing this is very important, because you can be very wrong in cash or bonds if you choose the wrong period, whereas the equity market history shows that over those same periods stock prices have outperformed greatly.

Using history as our guide, stocks outperform both bonds and T-bills. Therefore, looking at it mathematically, you can assume being in equities or holding stock in your portfolio is less risky than being in either bonds or cash. This, however, is not what the investment industry teaches. Advisers will tell us that bonds are less risk than equities. In the short term this could be true, but statistics show that on any 15-20 year rolling period equities outperform bonds and t-bills between 95 and 99 percent of the time, respectively.

With all of this in mind, your ultimate goal still has to be capital preservation and growth. So I like the odds of equities coupled with an understanding of market volatility, timing, and diversification.

Instead of looking at market volatility/EMH as an indicator of how much markets go up or down, we need to look at how much an asset outperforms other assets over the same historical time frame. If you look at inflation and deflation, the real risk is in the asset under-performing our needs for the future.

First, let's go into a more detailed understanding of the EMH. It has some other flaws. It assumes that an analyst's targets, estimates, and views are correct. Analysts are employed to assess a company and forecast their earnings. These analysts work for brokerage firms, and those forecasts and company evaluations are published and made available to portfolio managers, fund managers, advisors, and clients who are buying and selling stocks based on those forecasts. The problem is that according to the *Wall Street Journal*, analysts miss these numbers, on average, 80 percent of the time within a six-month period (two quarters).7

To compound the problem, analysts usually forecast up to five years, or twenty quarters out, which means, mathematically speaking, there is a 1 in 199,000 chance of an analyst being right throughout that period. I don't see this as an effective indicator for my portfolio selections. Yet, most advisers use this indicator to determine the price of the stock today and its future value. I do, however, think that an analyst's report on a company or sector provides insight and understanding and therefore should be a part of your analysis.

Analysts are also notorious for being overly optimistic. Statistics say that 65 percent of the time, forecasts are above the actual numbers when you look out more than three quarters.

We need to look at an analyst's projection as an educated guess; the chance that these estimates are correct is limited. An analyst has a tough time determining earnings for today, and the further out they go, the more difficult the projection becomes. Analysts do a great job, but it is important as an investor to understand how impossible their job is and how much value you or your advisor should put on their assessments. The estimates should be used as an overall guideline and not your only tool.

The other issue we have to look at when weighing the value of a stock indicator or an analyst's review is the political pressure they are under to favor or recommend certain stocks. Working in the business, I have seen analysts fired for negative forecasts and consequently sell advice.

One of the most lucrative arms of any brokerage firm is their corporate finance department. Here, they help companies raise capital by issuing stock, orchestrating mergers and acquisitions, as well as financing debt and equity. The fees charged for these services amount to millions of dollars for the firm's bottom line. A brokerage firm is the bank of the corporate world, but they also have the added responsibility of then trading that corporation's shares. Of course it would not be advantageous for a corporation that needs to raise capital to approach a brokerage firm that has a sell recommendation on their stock. Therefore, most firms have a core group of stocks, names that would always have a "strong buy" regardless of the price. If an analyst lowers their ratings, it will hurt their own corporate business.

In early 2000, just before the Internet bubble, of the 500 stocks in the technology index, analysts had a buy rating on 395 stocks, 37 strong buys, 68 holds...and guess how many sell recommendations? That's right—zero. Within one year, the tech sector had lost over 60 percent, eventually losing 85 percent in a two-year period. Great recommendations.

As a trader, it was common to have positions with the firm's money that were contrary to our recommendations for our clients. You can see the conflicting interests at work, and of course the firm will always win out.

Another flaw with the EMH is the bubble-and-crash effect. If stocks trade at the value they should, why do we have crashes and excessive bubbles? Markets move based on projections for the future. Sometimes stocks trade at eight times their earnings; other times they trade at twenty times their earnings. During late 1999 and early 2000, technology stocks were trading at five hundred and a thousand times earnings, and some of these companies were still in the infantile stage; some never did have earnings, just an idea. Many of these companies crashed, and their stocks went to zero within a year, which is anything but efficient. If markets were efficient, they would move up or down based on only the growth of the economy and corporate earnings, and markets would follow this trend until the growth stopped or reversed.

There have been thirteen so-called crashes since 1785, which is an average of one every seventeen years, always preceded by years of exuberance—periods of high leverage, high multiples on stocks or assets, which are then followed by fewer buyers at lower prices.

After reviewing the multitude of theories and models, working in the business from the inside, and spending the last fourteen years away from the minute-to-minute emotions of the market, I believe the best approach is the contrarian theory. Stay away from the curb, and avoid gambling with high-risk areas, or staying with a stock too close to the top and selling a stock too close to the bottom. The stock market is like a seesaw: as money goes in, the market goes up; as money comes out, the market goes down. The further it goes up, the higher the risk of it coming down hard.

By being a contrarian when there is exuberance in the market, you avoid the hard falls. Again, over the long term, good-quality companies are a must; however, they should be purchased when they are out of favor and sold when in favor. Stocks tend to gravitate back to the norm over time. Over three-, five-, and ten-year periods, this philosophy has proven superior.

A growth stock is one that has a high price-to-earnings ratio (p/e) and thus is in favor. Because investors are excited about growth stocks, a better than expected earnings number is anticipated, while a negative number would be devastating. On the other hand, a value stock, or one that has a low p/e and is out of favor, has an expectation of in-line or poor numbers. Because the stock is already out of favor, lower-than-expected numbers should not cause a further decrease, but better-than-expected numbers could move the stock much higher. Above-expected numbers for a favored stock, more often than not, will not affect the stock, because it was already priced in the stock.

Mis-pricing stocks is constant; therefore markets continually adjust, but are never at an equilibrium. If you want to be in the market at all times, I would suggest using the above strategy, and you will need to rebalance your portfolio continually depending on the movements in the market, and continue buying undervalued stocks and selling higher-valued stocks. Remember, quality stocks should not stay undervalued forever. I will talk in the next lesson about market timing and how to evaluate when to get in and when to get out. But either way, if you

are in the market looking for and investing in undervalued, quality stocks, you are taking a prudent approach to
your investments and reducing your risk.

*Wall Street is the only place that people
ride to in a Rolls Royce to get advice from
those who take the subway.-Warren Buffet*

LESSON 7:

THE SECRET—MARKET TIMING AND THE BUSINESS/ECONOMIC CYCLE

Be fearful when others are greedy, be greedy when others are fearful. —Warren Buffett

In life, there is a time and a place for everything. We don't have to follow the norm, but we do need to look at our situation and plan or alter our actions accordingly. You wouldn't buy a four-bedroom home for your family when you are eighty; you wouldn't start saving for your education fund at sixty-five; and you shouldn't cash in your life insurance policy for your retirement needs at twenty-five. You base these life decisions on timing, when things make sense for your needs. The market works in the same way. From as far back as the 1700s, when we started recording, the market has moved according to the business cycle. This cycle usually lasts between four and six years, which means you can expect it to go from the top of the cycle to the bottom and back to the top of the cycle within a six-year period.

THE ECONOMIC CYCLE

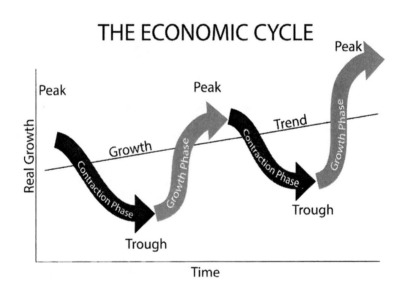

To fully understand the economic cycle, first we need to first look at its four distinct parts:

- Trough phase: low earnings, high unemployment, weak housing, few buyers, low interest rates

The Secret—Market Timing and the Business/Economic Cycle

- Recovery or growth phase: earnings rise, employment increases, housing prices rise, spending increases, asset prices rise, interest rates rise
- Peak phase: high multiples, low unemployment, high corporate spending, exuberance in the market, high number of corporate issues
- Recession or contraction phase: earnings decrease, unemployment rises, corporations slow spending, housing markets slow, sellers in the market

Markets move about six months ahead of economic data, which record what is happening in the economy.

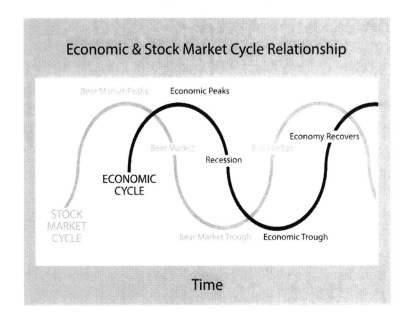

Economic & Stock Market Cycle Relationship

As we can see from the previous chart, indicators, such as housing starts, earnings growth, and spending, point us to the growth phase. This is the time to be fully invested. As growth moves to an unsustainable level, we get closer to the peak phase. There is exuberance in the market, and it is time to sell.

When markets correct, stock values and demand decrease, because the general populace is afraid to invest. This is the time to begin getting back into the market.

Almost all advisors and pension fund managers will recommend staying in the market. Regardless of where we are in the business cycle, they will say, "Buy and hold." The recommended industry formula for investing over any period is as follows:

X percent cash
Y percent bonds
Z percent equities

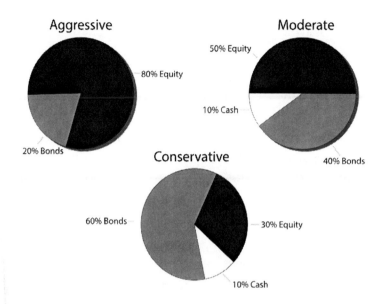

Aggressive

80% Equity

20% Bonds

Moderate

50% Equity

10% Cash

40% Bonds

Conservative

60% Bonds

30% Equity

10% Cash

Advisors will put you in a box and your specific formula will be calculated based on a decision by you and your advisor. Factors like your demographic position and risk tolerance will play the largest role, but the idea is to have more of your money in higher-risk areas when you are young and have the most time to grow your investments.

A typical model portfolio from the large firms is as follows:

- Younger client, higher risk: 80 percent equities, 20 percent bonds, 0 percent cash

- Midlife client, average risk: 50 percent equities, 40 percent bonds, 10 percent cash
- Older client, lower risk: 30 percent equities, 60 percent bonds, 10 percent cash

Some firms even use an age-specific method, which states you should own the percentage in bonds and cash equal to your age. Hence, if you are sixty-five years old, you would have 65 percent in bonds and cash and the balance in equities.

The premise of these formulas is that equities have the highest risk and highest returns, bonds are in the middle of the risk ratio, and cash has the lowest risk and the lowest return. When you look at this formula and discuss it with your advisor, it appears to make sense, along with their rationale to support this method. The problem with this generalized view is that they are missing the point of risk: real risk.

Should you be in 65 percent equities or bonds because of your age? Or should you be in 65 percent equities or bonds because of where we are in the business cycle? Let me give an example. As I write this in late 2014, interest rates are near zero. Here is an image of how low interest rates are at this point in time.

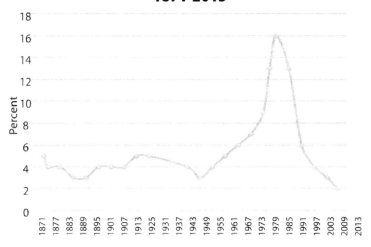

US Long-Term Interest Rates
1871-2013

Today, interest rates are the lowest in history. Bond prices go up when rates go down. Bond prices go down when rates go up (we have been in a thirty-year trend of lowering rates). I would say that given the chart above, the next move can only be that rates will go up. This means bond prices will go down; yet, almost every retiree and conservative investor is being told by the investment community that bonds are relatively safe. I shudder to think of what happens to that hard-earned retirement money that is in long-term bonds if rates do move up even 1 percent.

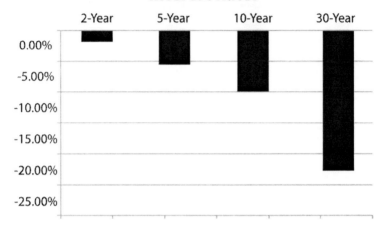

Price on Bonds of 1% Rise in Interest Rates

I believe your investment formula should be based on where we are in the cycle and the market's risk/reward and not on how old you are. Important issues, like market timing and hedging, are not considered, yet there are times when sitting in cash or owning bonds is much riskier than being in equities and vice versa. The investment community formulas are based on long-term market history; but as we saw with the housing and tech bubbles, there are times to be in and times to be out. This includes bonds and equities, because being invested all of the time means taking unnecessary risk regardless of your age. The following illustration helps to identify when you should be in each asset class based on the economic cycle

The Secret—Market Timing and the Business/Economic Cycle

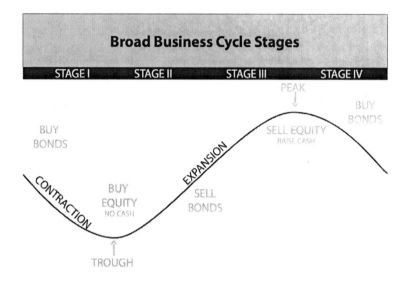

Unfortunately, when most investors discuss market fluctuation or possible future drops with their advisors, the theory that most are given is to look at the long term. Fund managers and advisors will show you charts that go back to the early 1900s and show you what happens to equities over a fifty- or hundred-year period. They will show examples of investing $1,000 in 1900 and what that return would be today if you had remained invested. However, most of us will not live to 114 years old. Other managers will show thirty-year returns, yet we invest the most in our late forties and fifties and are looking for fifteen- to twenty-year returns. Thirty or forty years is too long a horizon for most people. In any case, we need to be more financially savvy and risk averse with our economic future.

The boom years of 1982–2000 were some of the best years in the history of the market; it has been labeled as one of the all-time great bull markets. There was a very good reason for this phenomenon: it was the end of the Industrial Age and the beginning of the Information Age. Our society was beginning a whole new era. If we look back in history and compare the rates we experienced during that time with market earnings during other times, there is a huge deviance. Moves like those are generally followed by decades of slower growth and therefore lower returns. Yet, even during this spectacular time, there were major downward moves in the market. It is important to look at both medium-term (two to six months) and long-term (three to five years) trends. If you look over the last twelve years and you had just started your investment portfolio, you should have had good returns. If you are retired and used the "buy and hold" model, you probably watched your investments go down by 30 percent or more in the last few down markets, only to be roughly even now. The unfortunate part is that these drops were inevitable and foreseeable if you recognized and responded to market timing.

Stock prices move up in bull markets, which is when consumers and subsequently corporations are growing and spending and when too much money is running after goods. We are not seeing that today. What we are seeing is a Fed-induced market. The Fed is continuing to keep interest rates artificially low to generate growth at all cost. Current employment and corporate earnings can't justify the higher-than-average multiples in equities that we are seeing. Remember the tech sector when prices were five hundred times earnings. It is easy to see when you look back, but I think it is also easy to see possible risk when you understand the numbers.

You should base your asset allocation on economic indicators as well as market sentiment rather than staying invested in certain percentages in certain assets all of the time. You can maximize your investment earnings by buying when prices are low and selling when prices are high. While this sounds obvious, it is still contrary to the industry norm of buy and hold.

Your main goal as an investor should be to avoid the big moves down in the market, or at least part of them. You can't be right all the time, but it is OK to be too early selling or too late buying. You can avoid most of the corrections even if that means leaving some gains on the table.

Once you are aware of market cycles, trends, and timing, you can look for fear in the market before buying and look for greed as a sign to sell. Stocks are cheap at the end of a contraction phase and into a trough phase, but they are expensive at the end of the growth phase and into the beginning stages of the contraction phase. Buy when close to the trough; sell when close to the peak.

Most seasoned veterans will realize that when the market is looking expensive, they should reduce their risk by selling growth or high-multiples stocks like technology and consumer discretionaries. They will then move into more defensive stocks or those with lower multiples, like food producers and utilities. They will buy bonds when rates are falling and sell bonds when rates are rising. They sit with more cash when unsure or waiting for the trough.

These are very smart moves and ones that you can discuss with your advisor. The important part is to be involved and understand where and when you are invested.

Best Historical Performance In A Five Stage Cycle				
STAGE I	STAGE II	STAGE III	STAGE IV	STAGE V
UTILITIES		TECHNOLOGY		
CONSUMER		TRANSPORTS		HEALTHCARE
BONDS	BANKS	OIL DRILLERS	METALS	BONDS
CASH	TECHNOLOGY		ENERGY	CASH
	CONSUMER DISCRETION			

The Secret—Market Timing and the Business/Economic Cycle

As an individual, you are not required to stay in the market. You do not have to buy and hold a certain percentage at all times; this is the investment industries' way of keeping your money. You have the right and can choose to take your money out and stay on the sidelines during periods of high risk. *It is your money.* Historical data show that during the down times, even though fund managers moved to more defensive stocks, they still lost 40–60 percent. Firms like Investors Group, Royal Bank, Ontario Teachers, and Fidelity, who are trading millions of pension fund dollars, all saw their equity funds decrease by 30–50 percent during the extreme downturn only six years ago. These companies had mandates to keep your money in the market, and therefore, even when they saw the correction coming, they were unable to avoid the crash.

At the time of writing (late 2014), the market is almost six years into this bull market. There has been a 10 percent move up in the market already this year and a 10 percent gain in 2013 (very unusual considering very low inflation). Since the lows of 2009, investors have seen about a 100-percent increase (more in the United States with the Fed easing program to encourage growth). The average life span of a business cycle is between four and six years; the market is showing signs of being overbought and therefore, the risk of staying in the market is getting higher with each passing day. Stocks could go higher, but the risk of this growth cycle ending is mounting. Is it worth it to you to ignore the signs and accept what the market and your advisor will give you, or should you take control and understand the risk/reward at each step of the business cycle? In future lessons, you will be given the tools to further identify when to be in the market or a stock and when not to be.

It is up to you (or with a trusted advisor) to understand market timing and reduce your risk.

Bull markets are born on pessimism, grown on scepticism, mature on optimism and die on euphoria. The time of maximum pessimism is the best time to buy, and the time of maximum optimism is the best time to sell.—Sir John Templeton

LESSON 8:

THE MARKET AND EMOTION

*When everything seems to be going against
you, remember that the airplane takes off
against the wind, not with it.—Henry Ford*

"Buy the one with the bigger head and sell the other."
These were my trading instructions from a portfolio manager for me to buy $5 million worth of one company and sell $5 million of the other. The two intermediate-sized oil companies were in a court battle over who owned certain assets. The decision was critical to both. The portfolio manager was one of my best clients, and he couldn't decide what to do. So he threw a dart at the wall. We looked at the morning's *Globe and Mail*, which featured the two men and a commentary on the lawsuit:

"Pick the company with the CEO who has the biggest head." He rationalized that surely a bigger head would mean he knew more, and therefore his company would have a better outcome in court. That trade happened about twenty years ago, and I can't remember which way it went, but his process stuck with me. Even though he was an extremely successful portfolio manager, there were times when he, too, was just guessing. I was the trader, so I would still get paid for the trade. He was a fund manager, and he would still get paid. Of course, his performance was always being gauged. However, there were times when decisions were a shot in the dark with your hard-earned retirement money at risk. There isn't a fund manager out there who, at some point, isn't taking risks with pension or retirement money.

Like us, these advisors and fund managers are human, emotional, and not always rational in their decision-making process. When you purchase a family home or take a well-earned vacation, these trades better your life, and they should be emotional. Saving and investing are for later in life and should not be done with emotion.

SUPPLY AND DEMAND/FEAR AND GREED

As a company's revenue increases, sales go up, earnings increase, and there is more demand to own a part of that company. A positive fundamental change to the assets creates an increased demand for that asset.

When a government reduces debt and unemployment, but increases income through taxes, there is demand for that country's assets. This comes in the form of purchasing the country's currency and bonds.

On the flip side, if a company's sales drop, expenses rise, and revenues fall, or when a country has less income and higher unemployment, supply of their assets will increase and demand will go down.

By watching numbers such as cash flow or spending, earnings per share (how much money a company earns its shareholders), debt levels, capital expenditures, and consumer confidence, to name a few, we see how supply and demand for an underlying asset changes. This is how economists and analysts decide on a direction to invest. If this was the only influence, and there was no emotion in the equity markets, we would see a steady trend depending on the business cycle. However, humans evaluate and react to these numbers by guessing market and stock direction and reacting to outside influences.

Markets work on supply and demand, but are skewed by fear and greed. Remember the economic cycle chart? Well, here it is again, this time illustrating investor emotion within that cycle.

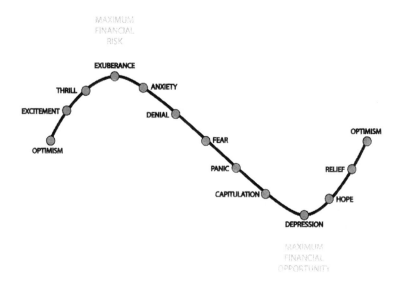

Active investors are price *makers*; they initiate buying and selling, therefore they drive the price of stocks up or down, creating new prices for the indexes to *accept*. Managers are human, with human emotions and needs. When emotion is used to buy and sell the market, our risk is based on the fund manager's mood, his or her likes or dislikes of management, the particular news he or she hears, and how much he or she listens to the trader on the other end of the phone. Or maybe he or she is fearful or greedy at the time. Either way, people are human, and human emotions lead to fund managers' decisions.

SCIENTIFIC DATA FOR MARKET MOVEMENT

Why do emotions play such a large role in market movement? Neurologists are working with economists to understand why we react the way we do to short-term news. They believe it is the allure of great profits and the excitement of a trade. Their research has shown that dopamine, which is a chemical naturally released by the body, is associated with the pleasure system of the brain. This system transmits impulses, which are released when reacting to a positive feeling. Sex, drugs, food, and even a trade all stimulate the brain. Of 100 billion neutrons, only 1 percent produce the chemical. When this chemical is released, the body responds positively. This is why someone on cocaine craves more. The brain wants that feeling again.

When dopamine is released, it gives us great pleasure, and we remember it and want to experience it again; it gives us a natural high. The truth is that this reaction is far more powerful than our fundamental cognitive thinking. The excitement of a great trade, a bet at the races, or another hit of cocaine has been proven to release the same reaction and can be more powerful than the logical part of our thinking.

As more studies are completed in the area of neuro-economics, the way we decide on risk, trades, and values may change. In the meantime, we need to remember that our view of risk is skewed. We have a natural desire to follow high-risk, high-multiple stocks.

I am not a psychologist, but through my experiences in the market, it is easy to see that the market is driven by emotional people who change their minds; they are not efficient, because humans affect the price of the assets, and humans are emotional.

People have strong likes, dislikes, and opinions. Happiness, excitement, and sadness are ingrained in our subconscious, and these feelings weigh heavily in influencing our decisions.

Feelings and opinions are much stronger and quicker to develop than our cognitive response or reasoning side of the brain. Emotion is at the forefront of our decision making. Whereas our cognitive response could take days or weeks, our subconscious opinions are instantaneous. We therefore make many decisions based on previous experiences rather than true facts.

As humans, we are also very insensitive to probability. It doesn't matter if the lottery ticket is a one in ten thousand chance or a one in a million chance, we still spend the same. The odds are bad, but the excitement of winning is greater than concentrating on the odds. Our judgment of risk is skewed. We believe that the higher the risk, the greater the reward. In stocks, the opposite is true: buying lower-risk stocks has proven to give higher rewards over time.

We tend to overestimate the short term. An announcement today changes our long-term thinking of the future. Government numbers will come out slightly negative, and the markets react by falling at the opening. All too often, at the end of the day, the market will close up. This is because those morning quarterly numbers didn't really change the big picture.

Stocks are mis-priced every day because of the human aspect of fear and greed. Following in the footsteps of other great investors, I like to sell when others buy and buy when others sell. The general public tends to react in the opposite way, with fear at the end of a sell-off and excitement and greed after a great market run. Markets become overbought and oversold in the peaks and troughs. Because investors don't want to miss out, they buy assets when everything looks great. Then when all looks terrible and prices are low, they sell. As Benjamin Graham once said, "The investor's chief problem—and even his worst enemy—is likely to be himself."

Fear is one of our strongest emotions. We want reassurance from our neighbors, friends, the media, and the powers that be to convince us that everything is good. We want to hear there is no downside; this is a great time to buy and we follow. Then, one day, just like dominoes, one person needs to sell, and does so at a discount. Before you know it, another walks away, unable to make his or her payments, and so on until there is a crash. Whether it is stocks, bonds, or houses, we tend to buy near the top and sell near the bottom. I'm not saying that one person can cause a housing market crash, but what I am saying is that you need to look at the pendulum and see how high it is when you are thinking of getting in or out of any financial market. If that pendulum is at all-time highs, you must be careful because you may have missed your opportunity and would be better to hold off until there is a correction.

We need to realize not only how quickly the market can correct or crash and the loss that can happen, but also the gains that can be had if we check our emotions at the door and look at stocks with our heads, not our hearts. On May 6, 2013, a trader at Waddell Reed accidentally sold 75,000 S&P Index futures contracts. The error occurred because of an automatic sell-and-buy program, and this sell caused a massive chain reaction. In less than twenty minutes, approximately \$1 trillion in market capital was wiped out. The market dropped a thousand points; stocks like Procter & Gamble (P&G) plummeted from \$60 to \$39.37, and a stock favorite 3M went from \$82 to\$68. A significant loss in two top stocks, and it had nothing to do with their fundamentals; it was a rogue trade. Was this a time to sell? Of course not. A few smart investors used this opportunity to step in and buy when retail accounts were selling out of fear. The market eventually closed down 347 points, although not before there was massive selling and loss—but only for the investors who sold in the panic. Those who watched the hysteria and took advantage of the opportunity capitalized on a terrific buying opportunity.

You can let the gamblers try to get the last of the market's tops and bottoms. During those high-risk times, every minute you are out of the market is time that you are avoiding risk. In the last thirteen years, there have been two major corrections with declines of over 50 percent. With risks like that, you can understand why "buy and hold" has become more like "buy and hope." With these sorts of hits to your savings and pension funds, you need long periods of growth like the 1980s and 1990s in order to make back the gains that you lost. The problem is that the future doesn't look good for this continued growth rate, which we've experienced since the 2009 bottom.

The tech bubble of 2000 was a time when investors in the new technology era were making money hand over fist, simply buying anything in this industry. Initial public offerings (IPOs) were up sometimes 50–100 percent the first day of trading. Investors weren't focusing on earnings; in fact, most of these stocks were reviewed for future earnings or the hope of what they might make. By 2006, the Internet bubble had burst, but people were leaving their jobs to buy real estate, holding two or more properties. Prices in Florida, California, and Arizona were at historical highs. It was euphoria, yet investors, home owners, and the Fed seemed to have forgotten the tech bubble a mere six years earlier. In fact, in 2006, the Fed assured the public that the housing market was safe; they saw no warning signs. Yet it was obvious that this rapid growth could not continue; market bubbles are created by high leverage and an exuberant, no-risk mentality that never lasts forever. Unfortunately, the people who finally jumped in because everyone else has are the ones who get hit the hardest. This takes me to the second part of the secret: buy low, sell high.

This does not mean to pick absolute bottoms or tops. To buy low is to purchase an asset when there is not a lot of other demand for the asset at that given time. To sell high is to release it when the majority of people love it. You don't need to be able to pick or call market tops or bottoms; however, you can determine if the stock is in or out of favor, just like you know Christmas lights at Walmart are cheaper in January than in December. Fliers will give you information about sales, and charts will give you information about markets.

When friends, family, the media, and, yes, your neighbour are all advising you to buy a stock, it's too late. The news is already in the stock. Let's think about this statement. They are already fully invested, and the only thing that can happen next is that some will sell. Who will the last buyer be? You? Once the expectations of the majority decrease and the stock begins to go down, more will now be forced to sell. Now is the time to look at buying.

This secret may sound easy, but for most investors, it is not.

The secret is to *understand why* and change your strategy to avoid following the crowd. Following the crowd means that you are at the back of the pack, and that's not a winning place to be.

The *why* goes back to the fact that investors are human. Buying and selling panics and extremes happen because of emotion, not because of the fundamentals of a stock, the market, or manipulation. They come about because markets are made up of individuals making calls on the market based on feelings.

To be able to buy low and sell high, you have to understand market cycles and what numbers affect it, turn off the hype, and avoid getting caught up in exuberance of market bubbles. You need to be in a position to buy when markets have corrected and are lower. Do not be afraid to sell when all others are buying.

The professionals are not so different when it comes to emotion, but they have the added pressure of the industry and what it is dictating. Can you imagine if a fund manager didn't have tech stock holdings during the height of the tech boom or if he didn't hold oil stocks when their prices were rising to all-time highs in 2013? One such institutional money manager was a client of mine. He had a very disciplined approach to trading; he never bought high-risk, high-multiple stocks. Then in late 1999 and early 2000, when the tech sector was booming, clients demanded they get into these stocks. The manager eventually caved to all the pressure causing him to lose those same clients the following year because of poor performance. He needed to stick with his plan and avoid the emotion; but of course in an industry that demands quarterly performance, this is not always doable.

You can avoid being fully invested at the top, and you can increase your positions when prices fall or when markets are at lows by using technical analysis as well as pure fundamental research to see market timing and cycles.

This is the real secret to investing: avoid most of the large downward moves, and be more heavily invested during the upward moves. It is far more important to miss the downward moves than to miss part of the upward moves. Let those with higher risk tolerance try to pick the tops and bottoms. The declines in your portfolio are harder to earn back than the lower returns on the way up. The head trader at Dominion Securities (the largest investment firm in Canada at the time) would ask me the rhetorical question, "When is 2 percent in cash a good thing? When everything else is losing money."

Most think of the world's best investor, Warren Buffett, as a buy-and-hold investor. In a 2008 *New York Times* article Buffett wrote, "If prices keep looking attractive, my non-Berkshire net worth will soon be 100 percent in American stocks."[8]

In 2007 his personal account held 100 percent US bonds, which made perfect sense: rates were dropping, and when rates drop, bonds go up. It was not until the stock market dropped 50 percent and became an extraordinary value that he sold all of the bonds and moved to 100 percent equities, which of course is a portfolio all based on market timing.

His corporate company, Berkshire Hathaway, took advantage of the market's decline as well by buying $3 billion worth of General Electric shares and $5 billion worth of Goldman Sachs when they were at all-time lows. Again, Buffett did not buy until prices were depressed and there was fear in the market.

One of my partners at Dominion Securities would say, "Feed the ducks while they're quackin'." If you are able to implement this mentality into your strategy, you will be at less risk and generate higher returns in the long run, but you will have to be patient. If there is one quote that sums up how to make money in the stock market, it is definitely not "buy and hold."

Be fearful when others are greedy; be greedy when others are fearful.—Warren Buffett

LESSON 9:

THE BIG PICTURE—WHY DEMOGRAPHICS MATTER

People do predictable things as they age.—Harry Dent

I'm getting tired of cutting the grass, building decks, and renovating houses. The house is too big, kids are heading off to college, and we don't need that four-bedroom house any longer. *It's time to downsize.* If you were born between 1939 and 1961, you are probably thinking this way. I was born in 1960, near the end of the baby boom generation. Demographic studies are seldom used properly by big government, municipal governments, school boards, business owners, and individuals, but they are a critical indicator for future population trends, growth, and needs. The largest and growing group in developed countries is the aging population, and this is followed by a smaller populace. For the first time in history, we have a smaller population following a larger population, which means fewer people to care for the aged. There will be a future increased demand on senior care facilities and needs associated with them.

Young people create growth and inflation. They spend money, they borrow, and they grow the economy. Older people tend to cause deflation because they spend less, borrow less, and downsize (sell).

There is predictability as to why the prices of private golf courses in the 1980s and 1990s were so high, why high schools were overflowing, and why universities continued to increase their acceptance standards.

People do predictable things at certain times in their lives, and demographics can show us where the majority and minority of those people are in that life cycle. On average, there are certain ages when we finish school, get a job, buy a car, have children, buy a house, buy a bigger car, buy a bigger house, buy a better car, retire, sell our house, move to a condo, and then rapidly spend less.

We borrow the most between ages forty and forty-four; we spend the most between forty-six and fifty-one. The last of the baby boomers, the largest age group in

North America, is about fifty-eight, so their peak in borrowing and spending has passed.

The next step is the downsizing and reduced spending, except in areas of health care, vacation homes, and cruises. They are not looking at big-screen TVs, minivans, SUVs, big houses, and furniture.

What happens when there are more sellers than buyers? We are left with a younger generation to bear the largest debt and highest housing prices in history as compared to their incomes. Yet, we are expecting them to make up the losses in our federal pension funds and our medical programs. This next smaller generation is expected to fund our retirement needs. It sounds crazy, and when you look at the demographics, it is crazy. This is another reason why I strongly believe you should take control of your retirement needs and not leave them in the hands of the government or the next generation.

History is one of our best teachers. Japan's demographic structure is about twelve years ahead of ours. Their largest population turned fifty-two in 1989, and a smaller population followed. That same year, the Japanese stock market index (Nikkei) peaked at 38,957 and dropped over 50 percent the following two years. Eventually, the Nikkei hit lows of around 7,000; it lost 85 percent of its value. There were, of course, other reasons for the drop, but we need to look at the impact the aging population had on the next twenty-five years.

From 1989 to the present, Japan has not experienced growth. It's had almost zero interest rates since the early 1990s; the government has continued to support the economy; and yet twenty-five years later, the market is still at half its 1989 value. Real estate prices fell by 80 percent two years after the market dropped and remain 60 percent below their 1991 values. In Japan, like in North America, population booms like other trends create bubbles. It takes many years to repair the damage caused once a financial bubble bursts. Therefore, we need to look at why there was one to avoid being part of the downside it creates.

Just like stock market and real estate bubbles, demographic bubbles are caused by too many people chasing the same assets.

Japan's 1989 demographics show that their baby boomers became non-spenders at around age fifty-two. So, no matter how much the government intervened, it could not change the lack of buyers for the assets that were for sale. Governments can lower rates to encourage growth, but they cannot create demand.

Consumers are 70 percent of the US gross domestic product (GDP). If consumers decrease spending, the economy will slow down. The US and Canadian baby boomers turned that corner in 2008; the past five years have been the final years of their large purchases. Thanks to massive government stimulus policies, the markets have continued and buying has continued, but this has been mainly by institutions and individuals with high net worth. We are now seeing the gap between the haves and the have-nots widen, but eventually this spending will give way.

As the major populace downsizes, supply will increase, and demand will decrease. Over the past ten years, states like Michigan, North Dakota, and Illinois have experienced outflows of people, while states like South Carolina, Nevada, and Washington, D.C. have seen inflows. Older people are retiring to warmer climates, and younger people are relocating to find jobs. The traditional manufacturing states such as Michigan and Illinois have fewer jobs, and in Canada the younger generation continues to move west and east for jobs. Traditionally, young people came to Quebec and Ontario for jobs; now, many are moving from those provinces.

Commodity prices can only head lower when worldwide demand decreases. Oil has peaked, as have almost all commodities. I would not recommend buying these assets at this time because they have further to fall in the coming years. They need to wash out the excess. The

Canadian dollar will continue to decline, probably below $0.75 in coming years because of our dependence on commodity prices. Canadian housing prices have risen dramatically in the past decade. Canada has one of the highest housing cost-to-income ratios in the entire world, and Vancouver is the highest in Canada with Toronto not far behind. Our personal debt levels are high, and we have not seen the correction in real estate that we saw in Europe or the United States. This would indicate that those corrections are still to come. I would look for real estate prices to drop by at least 30 percent or more over the coming few years.

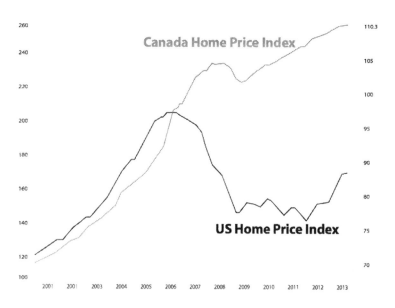

The majority of buyers, after the meltdown in the US housing market, especially in Florida, California, and Arizona, were the large US hedge funds. While a great number of Americans lost their homes because of foreclosure, they were purchased at very low valuations from the banks. As previously discussed, a hedge fund's mandate is to make money on any asset, and the bank's job is to loan money not own real estate. With this in mind, it is not surprising that independent estimates have hedge funds owning 40–60 percent of those foreclosed properties. Purchased at huge discounts in baskets by these funds, the majority of these individual homes are now rental properties. As the housing market has moved higher and these assets have increased in value, the hedge funds will begin to sell the houses that they purchase at the bottom of the market. This increased supply and limited demand could once again start the downward cycle.

We have not yet experienced a correction that puts equity prices in line with earnings. There are never booms without busts. Busts allow the market to realign with reality, flush out the excess and the greed. Only then are we able to rebuild and have long-term growth. By the time 2020 comes along, we should have experienced our major realignment as there will then be a stronger generation, ready to spend, replacing the decreasing number of baby boomers. We can then begin to move forward for longer-term growth. There are opportunities if you rely on the demographics and invest accordingly. Health care, anti-aging drugs, life insurance, cruise companies, RVs, and, yes, nursing homes are all areas that need to be on our stock portfolio's radar. India, Latin America, and the United States will be the first economies to improve. This is where the older and largest pools of capital will be going, and so should yours.

In the short term, we need to look out for a correction, pay down debt, be ready to buy assets when no one wants them, be risk averse, look at the big picture, and only then look at the intermediate term. When the baby boomers finish selling their assets, it will be time to buy. This group is supplying generation x, y, and z with product. Right now we are planning for the golden years. If you do not pay attention and prepare for this time, it may not turn out to be lined with gold.

Basic human principles don't change, but demographics and other circumstances do, and so should your responses to them. —Jon Kyl

LESSON 10:

TECHNICAL AND FUNDAMENTAL ANALYSIS

You have to learn the rules of the game and then play better than anyone else.—Albert Einstein

D o you want to be your own portfolio manager, or understand why certain stocks are recommended?

I have a litany of finance education—and, of course, my experience on the floor and owning a brokerage firm—yet, it is still tough to beat the market on a short-term basis. Active portfolio managers, certified financial analysts (CFAs), and a variety of other financial professionals are in that same boat: years of education and experience will not ensure financial success in the market.

But we can work with market timing and understand what we own and have a better chance, and that doesn't take years of study, just doing.

A study by Edgar Dale in 1969 stated that by actively doing something, giving a talk, or participating in a discussion, you will remember 70–90 percent of what you did in two weeks, whereas you will remember only about 10 percent by reading or listening to a speech.

LEARNING SUCCESS

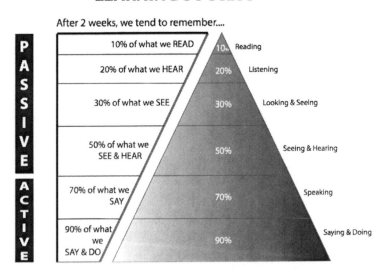

The best way to begin to understand trends and find out what works for you in the market is to have a virtual portfolio. This can happen on paper or on one of the many online apps available. Some examples of these programs are iTrade Simulator, MarketWatch.com/games, virtual investing from investopedia.com, or StockTrainer on Google.

STOCK ANALYSIS

Before you analyze a stock, you must think back to the big picture, the economy, and the market as a whole. What phase of the business cycle are we in? Is there growth in our economy, low unemployment, and inflation? Are rates rising? Would you say by looking at the housing market, price of food, or even your neighbor's renovations that we are in a growth phase?

On the flip side, are people thinking of selling their homes? Is there high unemployment? If so, we are in a contraction phase.

Just by looking around, you can gauge where we are in a cycle. You can go into more research, but just being aware will help you. The difficulty is knowing when it will change, but regardless, there are still times to be in different sectors depending on cycle positioning.

For example, if you believe there is fear in the market, and we are getting close to the bottom, the first stocks to move up are banks and technology. These are then followed by a rise in the energy, consumer goods, and the industrial sectors. When those sectors tire or show signs of weakening, it's time to trade into the more defensive utility and healthcare industries. The following chart appeared in Lesson 7, but I feel it is worth another look.

Best Historical Performance In A Five Stage Cycle

STAGE I	STAGE II	STAGE III	STAGE IV	STAGE V
UTILITIES		TECHNOLOGY		
CONSUMER		TRANSPORTS		HEALTHCARE
BONDS	BANKS	OIL DRILLERS	METALS	BONDS
CASH	TECHNOLOGY		ENERGY	CASH
	CONSUMER DISCRETION			

By following this path and watching these sectors change, you are able to follow the movement of the market and progress from lower-risk stocks, such as utilities (Bell Canada), to higher-risk stocks, such as consumer discretionary (retail stocks).

MARKET ANALYSIS

There are two ways to analyze the market, stocks, currencies, and all other financial products. The first is fundamental analysis; this deals with facts such as earnings, debt levels, cash flow, and so forth. This is how you are able to determine if a company is financially weak or strong. Is it growing? Is its debt level increasing or decreasing? This allows you to decide if one company or sector, or the entire market is above or below its conceived intrinsic value. The second is technical analysis, which assumes fundamental information is already reflected in the stock price; therefore, it uses historical price trends to determine the most likely outcomes. Technical analysis takes advantage of the psychological aspect of the market, whereas fundamental research looks only at the company's financial performance and future prospects, and then applies a target price to where they believe the stock will go.

FUNDAMENTAL ANALYSIS

Five key fundamental tools used by analysts to determine the price forecast of a stock:

1. Earnings

You want to know how much a company is earning today as well as its forecasted future earnings. This is usually denoted as price/earnings (p/e), which is the earnings for each common share. Over time, the Canadian market's p/e multiple averages thirteen to fourteen times, but growth companies can be much higher. A high p/e indicates that the price is high relative to its earnings, so you can assume this is a growth stock looking for higher, future earnings. A growth stock like Facebook trades at 140 times earnings, whereas Ford trades at nine times earnings. Therefore, Facebook has a much higher growth assumption than Ford, and has a much higher risk of not meeting future expectations.

2. Profit Margins

Earnings are important, but costs are equally crucial. Higher profit margins indicate that the company has better control over costs than other companies.

$$\text{Net Profit Margin} = \frac{\text{Net Profit}}{\text{Revenue}}$$

Evaluating this number depends on the sector. Technology and health care average about 15–20 percent, whereas industrials, utilities, and banks operate closer to the 10-percent level.

3. Return on Equity

Return on equity (ROE) is a ratio that indicates how well a company generates a return on its investments.

$$\text{Return on Equity} = \frac{\text{Net Income}}{\text{Shareholders' Equity}}$$

Overall, a ROE of 10 percent or less is unsatisfactory, 15–18 percent is good, and more than 20 percent is excellent. In other words, a 20-percent ROE means that for every dollar that is invested, twenty cents are earned.

4. Price to Book

Price to book (p/b) is used to compare the price of a stock to its book value—in other words, what the company is worth if sold today (intrinsic value).

A higher p/b ratio denotes that the share price is higher than the company is worth today if sold. The average p/b value over the past fifteen years has been about three, that is, the value of the company is worth three times the value of today's price, if sold. It is far safer to own a company that is at or close to its intrinsic value than to own a company that is priced many times its intrinsic value.

5. Debt to Equity

This is a measure of a company's financial ability to leverage. How much debt does it have compared to what it is worth?

$$\text{Debt to equity} = \frac{\text{Total liabilities}}{\text{Shareholders' equity}}$$

An automotive company may have a ratio above 2, whereas a computer company maybe below 0.5.

Generally, you want a low number to ensure there is not too much debt in the company. An exception can be a junior or start-up company that uses debt to create future earnings.

Fundamental analysis is a great starting point. The five steps above can help you pick the companies you are interested in, whereas technical analysis can help with your timing in that it deals with charts showing historical price patterns.

TECHNICAL ANALYSIS

Technical analysis is based on a belief that prices move in trends and are determined by changes in attitudes of investors due to fundamental changes that affect the price. It is an art to be able to identify a trend at a relatively early stage and ride that trend until the weight of evidence shows that the trend has broken.

Technical analysis uses charts under the assumption that all fundamental analysis is reflected in the price of the stock, that history repeats itself, and that because of human emotions, markets are not efficient.

Most technical analysis deals with momentum or the law of inertia: "a body in motion stays in motion." In other words, find the trend in a stock or the market.

There are two branches of technical analysis: market structure and sentiment.

I MARKET STRUCTURE

Trends

1. Primary trend: Four to six years (trough to trough)
2. Intermediate trends: Six weeks to nine months (or longer)
3. Short-term trends: Two to six weeks (these are far more random)

THE MARKET CYCLE

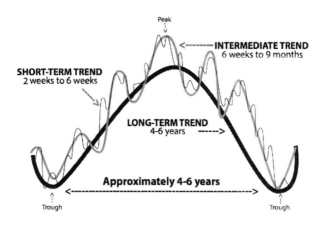

The primary trend is a link between the stock market and the business cycle. A business cycle trough to trough usually lasts between four and six years, while in general the stock market is about three to six months ahead. In other words, the stock market will bottom a few months before the business cycle shows signs of bottoming. So the price of a stock should decrease before the actual decreased earnings are revealed. On the flip side, if a business cycle shows signs of increasing, stocks should have increased three to six months earlier.

The idea is that if investors believe spending will increase, then productivity will also increase, and therefore profits will increase. This type of momentum is classic in a bull market.

Now you may be asking, "How can this help me when it shows only what has already happened?" The important point here is being able to identify the trends as you see them on a chart.

Technical analysis does not identify changes in corporate policy or the economy; it simply looks at the attitudes of investors toward these changes and how that transfers to the price of a stock. It identifies trends. Indicators like momentum and volume are also taken into account. If a stock is making new highs but only at the end of the day and volume on the stock is low during the day, then the stock should be viewed as being weaker than it appears and the movement to the upside will be limited. The stock's overall activity will not be viewed positively and will indicate more selling to come. It is a sign that the stock is getting tired.

There are other cycles, such as minute-to-minute trends, that are riskier and short term. There are also much longer secular trends. These are thirty- and eighty-year moves, such as the ones we had from 1934 to 2008. Within this secular bull market, there was a crash, a recession, and other times to avoid.

The technical analyst is basically a chart reader. He or she will use charts that are readily available for free on Yahoo, Google, Bigcharts.com, and many others. The first thing a technical analyst will do is try to identify the trend of the stock. Market structure looks at trends, market breadth, and volume. Trends are the most basic starting point for technical analysis. As stocks or indexes move, they will have support or resistance. In other words, people will want to buy or sell them at certain, identifiable prices. Once we identify a trend, we use other indicators to confirm our beliefs, and once the stock breaks the trend line, it will show a change in direction. The following is an example of a downward trend line followed by a new developing uptrend. As you can see, when the stock moves out of that downward trend, it is then time to buy, as a different trend appeared.

XYZ CORP. INTL (XYZ) NYSE · 3 YEAR CHART

Downtrend Line

Uptrend Line

Downtrend Line Broken

Jul · Oct · **10** · April · Oct · **11** · Apr · Jul · Oct · **12** · Apr · Jul · Oct

2. Moving Averages

Moving averages are the average price of a stock over a certain time period. A common practice is to plot a fifty-day moving average against a one-hundred-day moving average or for shorter-term charts use perhaps a ten-day versus a thirty-day average. When the two lines cross, it is a trend reversal indicator.

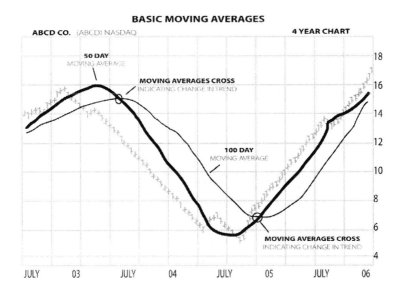

As you can see from the above chart, when the thick line (fifty-day moving average) crossed the thin line (one-hundred-day moving average), in July '03, the stock became a sell. When the thick line crossed the thin line in January '05, it was time to buy. As a note, the lines did not cross again, so you would still own this stock until the lines cross once more.

3. Moving Average Convergence Divergence

Moving average convergence divergence (MACD) plots the difference between two moving averages. As with simple moving averages, when the two lines cross, it is a strong signal to buy or sell.

The MACD indicator is the bottom portion of the chart. As the two lines widen, it is a sign of increased momentum. As those lines cross, it becomes a reversal in the direction of the trend of the stock.

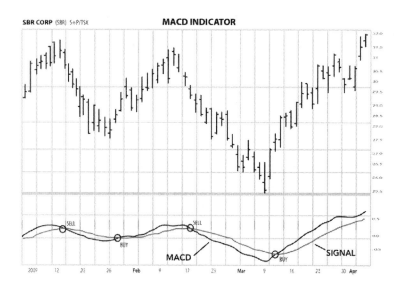

4. Relative Strength Indicators

Relative strength indicators measure the momentum of price movement on a scale of zero to one hundred. When the relative strength is above seventy, it is a sign that the stock has outperformed and is reaching an overbought position; when it falls below thirty, it indicates an over-sold position. The lower the number, the safer the risk, whereas the higher the number, the higher the risk.

Relative strength shows the momentum of a stock's movement. Momentum is the speed or velocity at which the price of a stock changes and the relative strength of the stock is determined. This speed of movement illustrates whether the stock is overbought or oversold as compared to its previous price history.

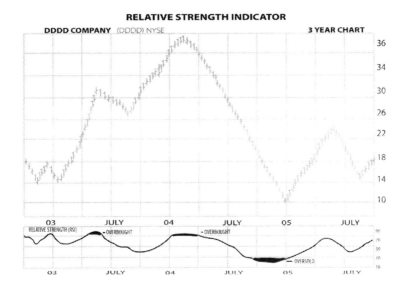

As you can see from the above chart, the relative strength indicator at the bottom of the chart told us to buy when below 30 and to sell when above 70.

5. Bollinger Bands

Bollinger bands are best used for shorter to intermediate terms. They are volatility curves that help identify highs and lows in a stock price based on past movement. They establish bands around the current moving averages, which help identify overbought and oversold positions.

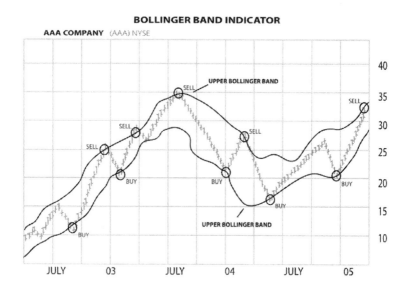

BOLLINGER BAND INDICATOR

AAA COMPANY (AAA) NYSE

As you can see from the above chart, when the price of the stock hits the lower band, it is oversold and is time to buy. When the stock price hits the upper band, it is overbought and time to sell, even within longer-term trends.

These charts illustrate just a few of the multitude of indicators that are available. Technical analysis is an art, and reading or studying charts can be confusing at first (it is a new language). However, the premise is simply to study past market and stock movements to determine future movements. While technical analysis identifies trends, it cannot determine when the trends will change. The main goal is to avoid losses and to identify when markets or stocks are higher or lower risk than in the past.

II. SENTIMENT INDICATORS

There are many surveys that help to determine the bullishness and bearishness of the market. These are very important because they reflect the attitudes of those investing in the marketplace. I look at these every month or two to get a wide overview of the sentiment of the general market.

1. *Investor Intelligence Survey.* This is published weekly and indicates a percentage of investors that are bullish or bearish. If the bearish reading is below 25 percent, then people are very positive on the market; if it is above 45 percent, people are negative on the market. This is a contrarian indicator, because as most people are bullish, it's time to sell. If most people are bearish, then it's time to buy.

2. *American Association of Individual Investors (AAII)
   Survey.* Every week the survey is taken and published. In the middle and end of 2012, the survey
   showed the lowest level of bulls in fifteen years;
   this was followed in 2013 by one of the best market moves up in fifteen years. The long-term average is 39 percent bullish, 30 percent neutral, and
   30 percent bearish. Extremes of 59 percent bullish, as seen in late 2013, are a good indication to
   be careful. Again, you are not looking to follow
   the pack but to see the human emotion and know
   when it is close to the beginning or end of a move.
3. *National Association of Active Investment Managers
   (NAAIM).* Active portfolio managers respond
   weekly to their range of positions, from 200
   percent short to 200 percent long (leveraged).
   Ratings in the eighties are average. Above one
   hundred is overly bullish. Under seventy is overly
   bearish. Again, a contrarian indicator.

Other sentiment indicators are consumer confidence
numbers (published by the government), insider buying
or selling, as well as short interest (both put out by the
exchange regulators), bull/bear market ratios (independent reports), and volatility.

Flow of funds is also important to review. This is
where we examine numbers of secondary offerings,

money flows in or out of bonds, emerging market funds, currencies, and overall equities.

While these indicators can be found on any financial site, I'd also like to share a couple of trading secrets that most people are not aware of (unless you are a trader). I found that when a market opened high, by lunch it was tired, and prices would start to come off only to resume again after lunch. The same is true when the market opens down. About two hours into the session, it reverses; then the selling continues after lunch. The idea here is that if people are negative, they sell. Then as the stock continues to move down at a slower pace, the seller does not want to continue to sell at the new daily low price, so he takes a break over lunch. Now the stock has moved up slightly, so psychologically he now feels better about continuing to sell. If you are a seller on a down day, execute your order between 11:00 a.m. and 1:00 p.m. If you are a buyer on an up day, then execute your order between 11:00 a.m. and 1:00 p.m. By doing this, you are going against the day's overall trend and should get better prices.

The same could be seen on four-day trends. As the price of a stock moves up each day (small first day, big on days two and three, then a little more on day four), roughly 85 percent of the time, the fifth day will see a reversal. Don't buy on day four; wait until the stock has had a day or two to settle back in before buyers are willing to purchase again. Do the opposite when selling in a down market. If you don't sell on day one or two in a down market, wait until day five or six. Stock prices are a reflection of human nature. When a price moves up quickly, people do not want to be the only ones buying; they want company. The investor takes a break to make sure he has support and that is reflected in the price.

None of these indicators are perfect. Technical analysis is an art, not a science. However, by weighing out the odds and understanding how people react based on the above indicators, your chance for success increases dramatically.

This lesson, while more in depth, is meant to allow you some basic understanding of the two main types of analysis. Use both. Once you set up the indicators on a typical chart program, which should take only five minutes, start exploring. Look up names you know, and see if you can find some trends—oversold and overbought stocks. You're on your way. If you have no idea or no desire, make sure that your adviser is using both types of analysis and that he or she understands them and implements them on your behalf.

Those who do not know history are destined to repeat it.—Edmund Burke

LESSON 11:

RISK—WHAT YOU HAVE NOT BEEN TOLD AND HOW YOU CAN INSURE AGAINST IT

October. This is one of the peculiarly dangerous months to speculate in stocks. The others are July, January, September, April, November, May, March, June, December, August, and February.—Mark Twain

You insure your house, car, and life; at times you also need to insure your investments. You can limit your risk, thereby insuring your finances, through timing. There are times to be in the market, and there are times to avoid it. From mid-2009 to late 2014, we have experienced five and a half years of a bull market, giving us a better-than-105-percent return. By November 2014, we were up 10 percent year to date. The business cycle only lasts an average of four to six years, so the odds of a market correction is increasing. Of course the U.S.government has artificially extended the market cycle, but the odds say that the market will correct soon. This means staying in the market at this point is high risk, and your probability of success is low. The odds are increasingly going against you. Economic indicators of consumer confidence, federal policy, exchange rates, and unemployment figures are all discussed regularly on market radio and TV, and they help us forecast the future. Watching numbers on a stock chart and identifying when it is overbought and oversold using technical analysis can help us in our assessment of the overall market. So, what can you do?

SITTING IN CASH

Any time you are invested in the market, be that stocks or bonds, is a time you are at risk. As we know, there are times to be in the market and times to avoid it. With a "buy and hold" strategy, you are always in the market, therefore always at risk. Going back to our lesson on market timing, the risks of being in the market when it is oversold are low; the risks of being in the market when it is overbought are high. The term *overbought* means demand unjustifiably pushes the price of a certain asset to levels that do not support the fundamentals. The higher the price rises, the greater the chance of a correction. This is a time when the rubber of the market is stretched to extremes. Gains in your portfolio are no longer based on the fundamentals, but on greed and investors fighting the odds. The more that elastic stretches, the more quickly and further it will come back. So why continue with the risk? It doesn't mean that the market can't go higher from here; no one knows just how far that elastic can stretch. You just have a better chance of higher returns when the market corrects, and there is an opportunity to buy into the market and hold it until the market becomes overbought again. This approach lowers your risk and provides peace of mind. Think about it: if you have reduced your exposure or are completely out of the market, you are now no longer at risk. Although I do not believe Treasury bills are great long-term investments, getting a little interest while you sit on the sidelines is much better than a decline in your investment.

When markets are showing signs of being overbought, let the other investors have the higher-risk gains. You can sell and sit in cash, risk-free, and sleep peacefully until the next time the market is oversold. Being truly risk averse sounds obvious, yet most advisors and a higher number of investors do not understand how to be risk averse or how to insure their portfolio.

During 1929, 1987, 2000, and 2008, the stock market experienced some of the largest percentage drops in history. Preceding all of these major declines was a bubble in equity prices, which clearly showed up in the charts. Unfortunately, the average investor, including retirees, didn't reduce their risk. As a result they experienced huge losses in their nest egg.

If you started investing in 1999 and had $10,000 invested by 2003, you would have had $9,125.20 less commissions and inflation.

If you followed the advice of buy and hold, "the market will turn around" mentality, by 2009 you would have had $9,381.65, but it would be less nine years of commission. It was a tough time for the buy and hold strategy. These, of course, are estimates based on what funds you were invested in, but you can see that the average person did not have great returns on investments for long periods.

During this same nine-year period, there were major up years and down years, and even up and down quarters (ten up and down moves of over 10 percent). If you followed the trends, you could have avoided some of the major moves down and realized double-digit returns by avoiding the major corrections. Unfortunately, the investment community doesn't suggest that you follow the trends and this type of investing philosophy, because once again this would be a money loser for them. There are always warning signs before periods of huge decline. Ignoring them is like standing in the middle of the highway waiting for the vehicle to hit you. When is earning 2 percent a good thing? When other investments are losing money.

DIVERSIFICATION

Diversification is another commonly misunderstood term. Having five balanced mutual funds is not diversification. Almost all balanced mutual funds have the same balance of cash, bonds, and equities/stocks. On top of that, they will all own roughly the same kinds of stocks and bonds in a certain sector. So, in essence, you have the same fund five times over. Owning Bell Canada in five different funds does not make your fund diversified. You need to have different stocks and bonds; you also need to look at different asset classes or sectors that have no relation to each other. Therefore, if one goes down, it should not have any correlation to the other. So if you own Petro-Canada in one mutual fund and Shell Canada in another, you are still vested in the oil market, whereas to be truly diversified you would hold a percentage of oil-related stocks and a percentage of tech stocks.

The suggested diversification model is to have five different asset classes; they can be in common equities, private equity, bonds, cash, real estate, gold and silver, or collectables to name a few in the most popular brackets.

We still, however, need to remember market timing and that there are good and bad times to be in each of these sectors and classes of assets (see Lesson 7).

I worked with a group that coined the phrase "optimal diversification." To diversify means to lower your risk by owning differing assets that don't move the same way. So if 50 percent of your portfolio is in the oil and gas sector, such as Petro-Canada, you wouldn't be advised to be in lumber stocks because these are both growth sectors. You would be better off balancing your investments by holding banks such as TD or Scotia.

Effective Diversification vs. Non-Market Risk

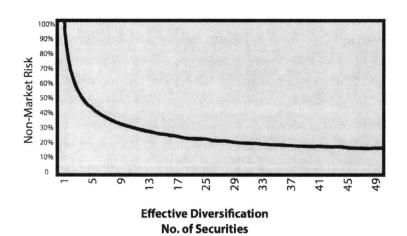

Effective Diversification
No. of Securities

Risk—What You Have Not Been Told and How You Can Insure against It

The previous illustration shows that as the number of holdings you have increases, your risk level decreases. However, as you reach fifteen to twenty holdings, further diversification does not substantially reduce risk.

Most mutual funds will own between one hundred and three hundred stocks, yet to effectively use "optimal diversification," you need only fifteen to twenty of the best stocks, and you can maximize your gains without increasing your risk, as well as understand and have the time to follow what you own. It is much easier to watch the movement of fifteen to twenty stocks (like hedge funds) versus one hundred to three hundred (like mutual funds), which means you can be involved with your portfolio. To see the maximum effectiveness of diversification, we used well-researched, quality stocks and ran them through historical data. By picking a variety of stocks in groupings of twenty and running them through past-performance analysis, we were able to see, quantitatively, the best approach to stock ratio versus risk. Our research showed that by adding more names to your good-quality, well-selected stocks, you dilute the value of your portfolio. By adding lesser-quality names, in order to reduce risk, you end up with an inferior portfolio, yet you were not reducing your risk rate by the same increments. We learned that optimal diversification for your portfolio offers the best chance for success.

The banks, fund managers, and advisors will have you diversify into a few mutual funds or a basket of mutual funds. They will tell you to buy and hold, keep averaging down, and stay invested at all times. I hope you can now see why this is not the best approach and is one that may be unnecessarily detrimental to your retirement.

HEDGING (INSURANCE)

On a recent trip to Calgary, I spent some time talking with a family member regarding her investments. Like most living in oil country, her holdings were heavily weighted in oil-related company stock options. Following the market trends, she could see that the market was overbought and was fearful of a correction. She could also see that her Halliburton shares (an oil drilling company) were at all-time highs. Past experience had shown that those investments had a higher risk of loss during times of weak oil prices, and she didn't want to watch her retirement plans take another nosedive. The challenge she faced was with taxes. If she sold her stock at the rate they were valued today, she would pay large taxes on her gains. She didn't want to cash in; she just wanted to avoid losing money if the market suffered another downturn.

Let's look at the ways she could hedge or insure against loss without having to sell shares, and have the possibility of making money from that position.

Risk—What You Have Not Been Told and How You Can Insure against It

1. Short Selling

The most effective way to hedge any position is to replicate 100 percent of that position in an opposite position. Let me explain. The typical way people think of trading is to buy a stock, which is called going long, and then sell at some time in the future. The profit or loss is the difference between the two prices. Obviously, when you go long, you expect the price to rise in the future. Shorting is the same in reverse. Instead of buying, you sell first or go short and then buy back the position later, preferably at a lower price.

Again, the profit or loss is the difference between the two prices. The natural question here is, "How do you sell something that you don't have?" The answer is, you borrow it. The process works like this. Let's say my cousin owns a thousand shares of Halliburton stock in her account. In a separate account, she would short a thousand shares, so she has to find a thousand shares to borrow. To do this, she asks her broker (advisor) to see if there are any shares available to borrow. If there are none, she's out of luck (which would be unusual). If there are shares to borrow, she simply puts in an order to sell short a thousand shares of Halliburton. Once that order is filled, she is now 100 percent hedged between her short account and her long account, no matter what way the stock goes. This way, she did not have to sell her shares but has insurance on them, and at some point she will have to cover her short position by buying back a thousand shares. During times of uncertainty she will be 100 percent hedged, her short position will increase by the same amount that her long position will decrease. You will, however, require additional funds to take advantage of a short position.

2. Inverse Exchange-Traded Funds

An exchange-traded fund (ETF) is simply a basket of stocks, like a mutual fund, that is traded on the market like a stock. It is meant to be a single product that covers or mirrors an index (Dow Jones Industrial Average), a sector (oil and gas sector), or even commodities (agriculture). If there is a sector or asset class out there, there is probably an ETF that mirrors the group. An ETF will move up in value at roughly the same rate as the asset class it represents. An inverse EFT is exactly the opposite. By using short positions or selling futures and options against the asset class, it can now perform inversely to the asset class. When the oil sector goes up, the inverse ETF will go down. When the asset class goes down, the inverse ETF will go up.

Let's go back to my cousin's dilemma. She wants to protect herself from the oil and gas sector's decline. If she felt the company stock was going to experience a downward slope in its value, then she could invest an equal amount in an opposing asset that goes up when the oil sector goes down, such as an inverse ETF, which covers the oil and gas sector.

Because an inverse ETF goes up at roughly the same percentage as the market or sector goes down, owning one would hedge her asset, which is what I like to call insurance. If the shares and the oil sector move higher, opposite to what she thought, she will be hedged and lose on the inverse ETF (insurance), but continue to make money on the Halliburton shares. If the Haliburton shares drop as she expected, then the inverse ETF will increase. She should hold this position until she feels there is no longer a need for the insurance.

Let's look at another scenario. If you own three bank stocks that have enjoyed strong dividends and you don't want to sell and trigger capital gains, or you want to hold on for the dividend, you still have options. In this case, you can buy a bank sector inverse ETF, which amounts to one trade, and you are now hedged at times when the market looks vulnerable. If the market declines to where you feel it is less risky than previously, you can sell the ETF at a profit, all the while continuing to enjoy your bank stock dividends and without triggering capital gains.

By protecting or even making money on your portfolio when signs are pointing to a correction, you can avoid the large losses and thus the risk. Remember, risk is not the same as volatility. You don't have to keep your money invested in the market all the time.

3. Options

Another source of hedging or insurance against an over-bought or oversold market is to use options. There are two types of exchange-listed options:

A. There is a *call* option, which gives the buyer the right to buy a certain number of shares for a certain time at a certain price. The seller of those calls is obligated to sell those shares should the buyer call them in.

B. There is a *put* option, which gives the buyer the right to sell a certain number of shares for a certain time at a certain price. The seller of those puts is obligated to buy the shares should the buyer put them to the seller (writer) of the option.

When you buy either option, a put or a call, you pay a premium to the seller for the right you have purchased, and the seller gets paid to give you that right. Equity options are sold in board lots (one hundred shares), thus one call or one put represents one hundred shares.

Types of Options

	CALL	PUT
B U Y E R	The **right** (but not the obligation to buy)	The **right** (but not the obligation to sell)
S E L L E R	The potential **obligation** to sell	The potential **obligation** to buy

Think of it as your ticket to the Stanley Cup. Your buddy owns season tickets, and you want to lock in your ticket for the playoffs at $100 each. So you pay $10 at the beginning of the season for the right to buy your playoff ticket for $100. If your team doesn't make it to the playoffs, you're out $10, but if they do make it, you can buy the now $1,000 playoff ticket for $100.

Back to my cousin who wants to hedge that Halliburton position. We can also insure her with options.

Choice #1: Buy a Put option

She could buy a put option. Remember, when buying a put option, you are purchasing the right to sell shares. Let's say she owns a thousand Halliburton shares, which are now trading at $40 a share for a total investment of $40,000.

For about $2,500, you could buy a put option, which then gives you the right to sell your shares at $40 a share for two months. If the stock goes down to $30 in the next two months, you will have a paper loss of $10,000 on your thousand shares. The option that you bought for $2,500 will now be worth about $12,500.

Halliburton shares	–$10,000
Cost of put	–$2,500
Sale of put	+$12,500

Net *loss zero* even though Halliburton shares dropped 25 percent or $10 a share.

These are theoretical numbers, of course. The price you pay for an option consists of two parts. One is the intrinsic value (what it is worth if exercised today), and the second is the time premium (you are buying this for protection in the future and are paying for that right). If the event happens soon, the time premium would still be in the option; however, if it happens at the end of the option period, there will probably be very little time premium, because the time has already gone by. The longer the time of the option expiry, the more time premium you pay. Options are generally short-term vehicles.

By spending a small percentage of what you own, you have now hedged or insured your position against what could have been a much larger drop. The above example was for an individual stock, but this strategy can also be implemented for your total equity holdings in one trade. You can buy a put option on the index.

If you are wrong, then your downside is that the stock continues to rise, and you lose your investment of $2,500, yet you have gained on your original position. Just like the car insurance you bought but never had to use—it still gave you peace of mind.

Choice #2: Sell a Call option

When you buy an option, you pay for it; when you sell an option, you get paid for giving that right to the buyer. As a seller, you have an obligation to sell the underlying asset to the buyer if the buyer wants it. Looking at Halliburton again, assume my cousin owns a thousand shares at $40 and wants to protect it at that price for a certain period of time. She could write (sell) ten (one hundred shares per option) call options for $2,500. The buyer of the option is paying her $2,500 for that right. She will, however, have an obligation to sell at $40 if the buyer of the call requests for her to sell. Let's look at the outcomes.

- She was right, and the stock declines to $35.

She never intended to sell the shares at $40, but now has produced $2,500 in cash from that position, which now lowers her cost from $40 to $37.50. She keeps earning on the position even as it is falling. If she thinks it will go further down, then she can write more options.

- She was wrong, and the stock moves to $45.

The shares that she thought would go down at $40 a share have gone up. She will now be forced to sell those shares at $40, but now has produced an additional $2,500 from the sale of the option, thus, realizing an equivalent sale price of $42.50 for her shares that she thought would go down.

This is an options strategy that can be used at any time to enhance the value you receive from owning an equity. This is called "covered call writing" and is used by many high-net-worth clients to actually create a form of income. This strategy allows this income to be taxed as capital gains and is much more efficient than income from dividends. If you own stocks, you can continually write calls and theoretically reduce your cost to zero over time; if the stock does move up you sell it, which is not a bad problem to have.

	Buy Call	Sell Call	Buy Put	Sell Put
Obligation/right	Right	Obligation	Right	Obligation
Pay or receive cash	Pay	Receive	Pay	Receive
Strike price				
(Halliburton)	$40	$40	$40	$40
Cost for one option				
(100 shares)	$400	$400	$400	$400

Price will represent intrinsic value + time premium.

Most fund managers and advisors do not hold an option license. Options do, however, provide great insurance as well as income and, yes, choices for you in sideways, difficult, or risky markets to make money. So I would encourage you to find a manager that also has this license and can discuss using these formats in your portfolio.

4.   Stop Loss Orders

Remember our targets and goals section. You should always have targets for your equity positions. This not only means how much you are looking to gain, but more important, how much you are willing to lose. A way to protect capital and limit losses is to use an on-stop order. This is an order to sell a security at a certain price when the requested price is lower than the market price. Let's say you buy a hundred shares of Halliburton at $40. You believe the shares will go higher, but are not willing to lose more than 10 percent if you are wrong. Immediately, after purchasing these shares, you can enter an on-stop order to sell a hundred Halliburton shares at $36, which is 10 percent of the shares' value. If the shares reach $36, your order becomes a market order to sell. If this happens, you have limited your liability and risk of loss to $400 (the 10-percent risk-tolerance level).

We also need to guard against gains so that we don't over-invest or become greedy. This type of strategy will allow you to avoid a situation where your stock goes up, and you are thrilled, forget your target price, and get greedy...only to then see your profit disintegrate before you can react. Let's say you have a target of $45 on your purchase of Halliburton. The stock is doing well and is now at $45 a share. You believe it will go further. You can now put in an on-stop order to sell at $43 to ensure you at least keep some profit. If the stock continues to move up to $47, simply change your on-stop order from $43 to $45. By using this strategy, you will never sit by

and watch a profit turn into a loss. Not only does this
make sense financially, but emotionally you will not have
to ride the market roller coaster.

Using these investment tools makes investing in the
stock market much safer. These options provide safe insurance, don't cost much, and yet they give peace of mind.
Like all insurance, it is great to have it when you need it.

As you consider each of these options for insuring
against risk, you're probably wondering how you'll know
when or if the markets are going to continue going up or
down. You won't know this. None of us has a crystal ball,
so you won't know if the markets are going to rise or fall,
just like you can't predict a fire or tornado. However, you
can ensure that you have fire extinguishers, smoke detec-
tors, and insurance, and you can watch the news from the
safety of a shelter. It is the same in the market: you can train
your eye to see the charts, listen to the news, and know
when markets appear overbought and oversold, and then
you will be able to determine if it is time to insure your
holdings or not. When equity prices rise 100 percent in six
years, including 10 percent last year while earnings growth
is below 3% and consumer confidence is high, chances are
it is time to do some investigating and insuring.

The idea remains to protect your asset, don't gam-
ble with your gains, play safe, and to avoid and insure
against the risk.

I'd like to recap the main ideas in this lesson
RISK INSURANCE:

1. Sit in cash
2. Diversify
3. Hedge
    i.   Sell short
    ii. Inverse ETF
    iii Options
4. Stop orders

Using derivatives (options and futures) is common practice among investors like Warren Buffett, hedge fund managers, and high-net-worth investors, but it can be done by anyone. As a side note, reportedly 30 percent of Berkshire Hathaway's quarterly earnings came from derivatives, which amounts to hundreds of millions of dollars.

While these insurance suggestions are not foolproof, they are just like home and life insurance. They are put in place to cover you against a wipeout and provide peace of mind.

It's not whether you are right or wrong that's important, but how much money you make when you're right and how much money you lose when you're wrong.—George Soros

LESSON 12:

TAXES MADE SIMPLE

The hardest thing to understand in the world is income taxes.—Albert Einstein

If an accountant's wife can't get to sleep, what does she do? She leans over to her husband and says, "Tell me about your work today, honey."

Taxes can be boring, complicated, and very frustrating, but ignoring them could be detrimental to your financial health. The cost of a good accountant is invaluable in your efforts to maximize your investment income as well as your net income.

Taxes are levied in this order:

~Regular earned income and interest income—highest
~Dividend income—middle
~Capital gains—the lowest (you also deduct capital losses against your capital gains)

For a couple, one of the most effective ways to minimize your tax exposure is to have the person earning the lowest income hold the interest and dividend income and have the higher-tax-bracket person hold the capital gains, thus resulting in overall lower taxes.

If you have capital losses, you deduct those from your capital gains (allowing you to have less capital gains to claim than you would have). If you do not have any gains that year, you cannot use the capital loss that year on your taxes; however, you can use the losses going back three years and an indefinite number of years forward.

DEFERRED TAXES

Registered Retirement Savings Plans (RRSP)
Would you rather have $1 million in your Registered Retirement Savings Plan (RRSP) or $1 million in a non-registered account? The RRSP will be taxed when you take the money out, even in retirement. In other words, what you think you own in your RRSP is not all yours. You have a partner—the government. Let's say your pension income is $50,000 a year, which includes your Canada Pension Plan income and your personal withdrawal from your retirement fund. Currently, you will be taxed at a minimum of 32 percent, and who knows where that figure will move in the future. This means

that the $1 million you have for retirement income is really worth under $700,000. Every dollar you put into an RRSP and every dollar you earn in your RRSP will be taxed when you take it out. RRSPs are great short-term plans to reduce taxes now, but you need to consider the future. The only way to protect the money you have put into your RRSP is to use the tax refund as savings instead of spending money. These funds *must* be invested in a non-registered account to grow and cover the costs of the taxes that will be owed at a later date.

It is a good idea to use the tax write-off for your RRSP savings in earlier high-income years, but you need to be careful in how you are taxed when it is time to use that money. Rather than consider this tax refund windfall as income today, you need to use the refund for investment purposes for your future.

Spousal RRSP
The idea behind investing equal amounts in your RRSP and your spouse's RRSP is to even the tax burden when you take money out. If one of you is taking out $60,000 per year and the other isn't taking anything out, the tax rate will be higher than if both of you were taking out $30,000. This lower tax bracket that you and your spouse develop can amount to thousands of dollars during your retirement years when you don't have thousands to spare.

Non-registered Account
You also need to look at the best place for growth within your investment vehicles. Different plans are designed for different purposes, and they have different tax implications. You want to have higher capital gains inside your non-registered plan as opposed to your registered plan (RRSP), because a non-registered plan will be taxed at the lower capital gains tax rate. Then it is taxed between 19 and 23 percent, depending on your income.

Let's break that down. If you have a $300,000 gain in a non-registered account, you would pay taxes bases on it as a capital gain. If you are in the middle-income scale range, then the capital gains would be in the 15-percent range or $45,000 (the formula is capital gains divided by 2, then taxed at 30 percent). So after you pay taxes, you would keep $255,000. On the other hand, if this gain was in your RRSP, when you take money out in future years you will be taxed as if it were income at that time. So at the time of withdrawal, you would pay the highest marginal rate of tax, which would mean 46 percent in Ontario. Therefore, when you withdrew this gain from your RRSP, you would pay $138,000 and would keep only $162,000 after taxes.

Canada Pension Plan
Tax implications also need to be considered for your pension fund income. The Canadian Pension Plan is a

mandatory tax-deferred vehicle, and funds are taxed when they are received. The monies that you get will be added together along with your RRSP and Registered Retirement Income Fund (RRIF) income to determine your marginal tax rate.

MINIMIZING TAXES

Family Trust
A family trust may be another option. By putting assets that create any type of earnings into a trust, you are able to split the income among the beneficiaries. For example, you put an asset that grows by $60,000 a year into a family trust. It would then be taxed equally between the beneficiaries and not in your hands. It does mean another tax return form to be filed on behalf of the trust. However, the taxes would be split and claimed by the beneficiaries at a lower tax rate. If you had three children in the trust, they would each claim $20,000 on their taxes. It may seem like too many tax returns, but you are sharing your earnings and splitting the income away from you. There is a catch, however: the trust owns the assets listed in it, and the beneficiaries are the true owners of the assets.

Small Business
If you own a small business or contract your services to others, you should income share as much as possible. By

employing your spouse and/or children, with legitimate pay for legitimate work, you are able to share the income and the tax load. Before taxes are paid in your business, you can also pay for insurance products with pretax dollars as a business expense and reduce your company's tax load. You can also purchase a personal small business pension plan from your company. The earlier you start, the faster it grows and the more you save, both through tax relief and investment gains.

NO TAXES

Tax-Free Savings Account
One of the best Canadian tax vehicles is the tax-free savings account (TFSA). This is where you want your big capital gains. In 2013, you were allowed to put in $5,500 and the four previous years $5,000. It is not just the $5,500 you put into this account that is the big deal for retirement, it's that whatever gains you make on this account are tax-free. So if you have been putting money into this account each year, you should have $25,500. Let's say you earned $100,000 on this money, over time you can withdraw it anytime without paying any taxes! You can earn income, dividends, or capital gains, but you never pay taxes on them. The idea is to put your money

into this account after taxes, and therefore nothing will be owed. Here is a simple comparison between a TFSA and an RRSP:

	TFSA	**RRSP**
Pretax income	$1,000	$1,000
Tax	$400	N/A
Net contribution	$600	$1,000
Value in twenty years at 6 percent growth	$1,924	$3,207
Tax when withdrawn (40 percent tax rate)	N/A	$1,283
Net Withdrawal	$1,924	$1,924

Although both of these accounts look the same, they are only the same if you earn simple interest. If you have capital gains, the TSFA is a hugh advantage. You need to make sure this tax-free account is used optimally, and in the end it will be your money and not a profitable investment that you share with the government. Any withdrawals from this account are not added to your income, registered or otherwise, and therefore it is not taxed. If you are obtaining substantial capital gains, I highly recommend the TFSA over the RRSP, because those gains will be completely tax-free. It will make a substantial difference in the end.

Registered Education Savings Plan

One other great tax haven is the Registered Education Savings Plan (RESP). If you have children and you expect them to go to postsecondary school, an RESP is a must. The government will give a tax-free grant along with your deposit. For each child, there is a 20-percent grant up to $5,000. In other words, you put in $5,000 per child, and the government will grant $1,000 per child up to a maximum of $5,000. This has to be the easiest 20-percent gain you will ever make. Of course, if you do not use the money for postsecondary education, you will owe the grant money back. But if you have more than one child, the grant money is interchangeable. So if child A decides not to go to university, but child B decides to get a master's, you can use all of the money on child B and not owe the government anything. This program also allows you to make a one-time top-up, which helps if you haven't been making payments through the years, but would like to take advantage of the program.

Real Estate

Your home is probably the best tax-free vehicle available. It will generally appreciate over time, or you have the opportunity to make improvements to help with the appreciation, and you pay no capital gains on your profit.

Real estate that you own but is not your primary residence, such as an investment or second/vacation property, is taxed as a capital gain, but at a much better rate than earned income or the dividend tax rate. Any gains from the sale of that property incurs taxes on the profit (however, at a lower capital gains rate).

TERM INSURANCE

Term insurance is insurance for a certain term or period, and when its term is up, it expires and you get nothing (like house or car insurance). Term insurance should be used when you have an obligation to fulfill in a fixed amount of time.

For example, if you are a single parent with a ten-year-old, and you started saving to have $100,000 in eight years for his or her education fund, you might be concerned about something happening to you before you reach your goal. In this case, you should purchase a depleting term insurance policy that will deplete as your savings increase. This way, if something happens to you, your child will still get the education fund.

PERMANENT LIFE INSURANCE

Another vehicle for investing is through an insurance product called whole life. One of the best investments I have ever made was to buy a whole life insurance policy. Not only does it offer increasing life insurance, but it is also a creditor-protected and tax-free investment vehicle. The cost is higher than term or straight life insurance, but because these added premiums go into the investment side of the policy, it will have a cash value. You can surrender the policy at any time and receive this cash value; you can borrow a portion of the cash value from the insurance company; or you can use the policy as collateral for a loan at a bank.

Insurance payouts are given directly to the beneficiary, and, therefore, he or she avoids a tax called probate fees. Also, any assets that you own, upon death, in any type of account that are not assigned to a specific beneficiary will be subject to this probate fee. This could be a major liability to your beneficiaries. I see investing in this type of low-risk, lower-return product as the "mattress policy," with the added bonus of providing my family with life insurance.

Yes, I was a trader. I believe in market timing, I believe in maximizing my returns, but I don't believe in risking everything. I believe in balance. Insurance won't give spectacular returns, but it will be there, and it will help you sleep at night.

You may hear that you shouldn't mix insurance and investments. However, I think you have to go back to the concept of your paycheck and whatever money is leaving your paycheck needs to be part of your formula. What is the best place for each dollar? What is going to provide the best tax relief so that I have the maximum amount to invest? What is going to give me the best return on those investments? What is going to give me peace of mind and balance? The reason you have bonds or cash allocations in a portfolio is to reduce the risk in the equity market. Why not use those bond and cash positions in your port-folio and transfer them to an insurance asset? By put-ting your safe allocation under an insurance umbrella, you get the added benefit of having an insurance policy that is backed by bonds and cash. You will now have your bond/cash position in your portfolio, and it will provide insurance. Insurance has a guaranteed growth rate, which is higher when markets are strong and the cash value does not decrease.

If you are ever sued, this policy can never be touched, as it is outside the courts and is creditor protected. When you die, the funds are sent directly to the beneficiary and do not go through probate because they do not go to the estate.

When I purchased the whole life policy many years ago, I did not fully understand how beneficial it would be. I put in a large lump sum every year. Today, it not only gives me the insurance I need, but also a cash value that grows every year. It is my bond/interest-bearing portfolio, but I don't have to fret about the bond market returns because my cash value can never go down.

*You must pay taxes, but there's
no law that says you gotta leave a
tip.—Morgan Stanley advertisement*

LESSON 13:

PICKING AN ADVISOR

A smart man makes a mistake, learns from it, and never makes that mistake again, but a wise man finds a smart man and learns from him how to avoid mistakes altogether.—Roy H. Williams

It took two years for a financial advisor in Calgary to finally get my wife and I to sit down at the other side of his desk. I was working in the stock market and saw no reason to sit down with a financial advisor. I was making more money than he was, and I was too young to think about retirement. In my view, an advisor was only going to talk about life insurance or other money grabs that would never satisfy my investment return expectations. Like all good advisors, he didn't take my putoffs as a no, and he continued to call. Thanks to a partner of mine, I finally had that first meeting. Once we started talking, I quickly learned that I may have been making more money, but I wasn't doing a good job of putting it in the right pockets. He was going to have a much better retirement than I. Not only was it not too early to meet with him, but it was also almost too late.

At thirty-eight, I had catching up to do. Had I even spoken to him two years earlier, when he started calling, I would have been in a much better retirement position. The lesson was crystal clear: you need an advisor when you start working, not when you are ready to finish working. After spending time with Tom and his business partner, Alison, I realized for the first time what the implications of not planning for retirement early enough could mean to me and my family. I never thought about being sixty, let alone eighty. It was time.

Luckily, during those first few visits and all the discussions for tax relief and where to put our money, rates were much higher than today. It took many visits and hours of reflection to set goals, but in the end, we thought of our advisors as friends. We learned to trust them, learn from them, and work with them. We had spoken to people who had branded themselves as financial advisors in the past, but the fit was wrong, and frankly, they turned us off from the industry because of their lack of knowledge. Our advisors were knowledgeable about all elements of investing, tax relief, and planning, and they were happy to offer outside expertise to assist in the execution of our decisions. They were the best fit for us.

Today, Tom and Alison are friends who have been there for us through midlife retirement without a financial monkey on our backs.

Most of the people who talk to me about their finances say the same thing about their advisors: "He calls only once a year asking for more money to put in my RRSP."

This is not good enough, and I hope those advisors are short lived in this environment. You deserve better, no matter what your financial plan or status looks like. It's your money, and you are paying for their services. I would suggest sitting down with two or three prospective advisors and interview them. Ask about their investment strategies, beliefs, what they can offer you and why. Ask about different investment vehicles, like those we have talked about in this book. Pick which ones you think make sense for you, and ask the advisors their thoughts for your portfolio. Then you decide who the best fit is for you and your future. Do not be afraid to ask questions, and do not allow them to talk in a language you do not understand. You must leave feeling comfortable and truly understand how this new relationship will benefit you.

Here are some qualities and areas of expertise that you could look for in a good advisor.

TRUSTWORTHINESS

Trustworthiness has to be number *one* in any partnership. If you cannot believe the words that come out of your advisor's mouth, what is the point of listening? You should never have doubts about what your advisor is saying. While you may not agree, you should not have to question his or her ethics. You are entrusting your advisor and paying him or her for this service. Their fiduciary responsibility is to put you and your money above everything. The number one rule as an advisor is the KYC rule—know your client. All of the information they share with you is to be true, plain, and fully disclosed. When you talk with an advisor, there should be no hidden agenda or persuasion. Always ask around to find a good advisor. Interview candidates and then check their references like you would with anyone you were hiring for an important job. After you have narrowed down your search, spend an hour with your potential advisor. See if this person feels right for you and your family. Ensure this person is someone you trust and feel comfortable working with openly and honestly.

LIKE YOUR ADVISOR

This does not mean your advisor has to be your best friend on Saturday night. What it does mean is that your advisor should have the same core values and beliefs that you do and that you have mutual respect. It is very difficult to work with someone you genuinely do not like and respect, even if that person is good at his or her job. If this advisor is hard to approach, talks beyond your knowledge, confuses you, or makes you feel uneasy, then you may need to look for a better fit. You need to feel completely comfortable asking questions; you need to understand how the advisor is investing your money and getting paid. Remember, you are paying a fee for the service. Whether you see it or know about it, the fee is there.

KNOWLEDGE

Formal education and knowledge are not the same thing. Higher education is great, but having true knowledge of how markets work and what to do with your money is more important. An advisor must share that knowledge in plain, usable language that doesn't boggle or confuse.

You want an advisor who can help you understand the variety of investment vehicles available, tax implications, market fluctuation, and timing. An advisor needs to develop a financial life plan with you, a plan with targets, time lines, and benchmarks—ones that you can see and follow and adjust as investments change or don't work out.

Most advisors have in-house products. If these are touted as the best vehicle to fit your criteria, they should be compared with other available options and offered for review. If this is not happening, ask the advisor to explain the philosophy of the product and provide options or alternatives. There should never be a reason for you to feel confused or pressured into buying an investment. Remember, you will have to live with the effects of poor advice, not your advisor. So you need to be able to gauge the success or failure of these investment products on a regular basis.

ALTERNATIVE PRODUCTS (OPTIONS, FUTURES, INSURANCE, HEDGING)

Hedge funds, options, and hedging your account are all things you should understand when you are invested. Whether you use these alternatives every day, once a year, or never, having an advisor who is registered in these areas and understands how they work is a benefit to you.

Does your advisor know that markets are up 65 percent of the time and down 35 percent of the time? Does he or she believe there are times to be exposed to the risks in the market and times not to be? Does he or she understand there are times when assets like stocks become liabilities?

I'm sure your advisor wants to help you, just like a mechanic wants to fix your car. The question is whether he or she has ever worked on your model. Then the question becomes, how vast is his or her knowledge? The investment community, including the regulatory bodies, are adamant that buy and hold is safe. As a result, most advisors recommend this approach. Your job is to choose an advisor who understands the investment choices he or she is offering and the possible ramifications of the market on them, so that you are consciously putting your money in the pocket best suited for your goals. The intent of investing is to make money and certainly not to lose your money.

RISK AVERSE

Does your advisor believe that capital preservation is of utmost importance? You want ideas and recommendations that help you reach your goals but without excessive risk. Within the KYC rules, you will sign a form that ranks your risk tolerance. The advisor should lean toward preserving capital. Make sure his or her short-term investment ideas are in line with your long-term goals. Make sure you and your advisor are on the same page.

FEE BASED

Currently, 80 percent of retail advisors in the United States are now on a fee-based service only. Canada is about 60 percent, but this number is growing. This means that by using this structure, you and your advisor are on the same page. For the first time in history, the advisor will make no more in fees with fifty trades than he does with five trades. Almost all high-net-worth clients follow a fee-based structure, where they pay a set yearly fee for everything as opposed to different amounts for different services.

I prefer this approach. Because you understand up front what you are paying for, it creates transparency. This enables the advisor to be on the same side of the table. The fees usually range from 1 to 3 percent, depending on the reputation and value of the advisor.

NOT A ONE-TRICK PONY

With some firms, the only products an advisor is allowed to sell are those of his or her own firm. In other words, the advisor has very few products he or she can advise you to buy. This is very limiting, and you may have to choose a different or an additional advisor to find the products that best suit your needs. Today, the large Canadian banks have opened their doors to allow the sales of most competitor's products, which means a bank advisor can assist you in purchasing or investing in another bank's products; they do this because it is good for their clients. However, some independent firms still have their hands tied and can only sell their own products, and these products cannot be purchased by other advisors for their clients.

FULL DISCOVERY

Gone are the days of a separate insurance, stock, and bank broker. It is much easier for you as the client to have a licensed wealth manager or investment advisor who can discuss all aspects of investing and your future. Many advisors have completed the long, arduous road to be certified in the variety of investment vehicles discussed in this book. Check when you are looking for your advisor, and ensure they are registered under the Investment Industry Regulatory Organization of Canada (IIROC) and not just the Mutual Fund Dealers Association. IIROC is a highly regulated organization that ensures advisors are proficient, monitored, and effective in the art of investing in the market. It is important for your portfolio and for your protection.

Be sure your advisor also takes the time to go through a complete financial discovery process with you. This gives the advisor a bird's eye view of your finances and life goals, better enabling him or her to implement a plan to help you reach them. Not only is this important for the advisor, but the process also provides you with peace of mind. By documenting your information, you are forced to take a good look at the present and what you need for the future.

Spend the few hours; it is worth it.

If you don't know where you are going, any road will get you there. —Lewis Caroll

CONCLUSION:

PUTTING IT ALL TOGETHER

You are never too old to set another goal
or to dream a new dream. – C. S. Lewis

By now you should know I am a contrarian when it comes to investing and life. Some of you are just starting out, or you are on the upward trend in your career; you have time to create wealth. Some of you are wrapping up and ready for retirement. My views and strategies are equally important to all groups. Understand what you have and what your goals and targets are for life and finance. Find a good advisor, one who will help you develop and implement your plan and understand how to work with you and your investments to maximize your financial portfolio and minimize its risk.

I hope this book has taught you how to be involved and connected to your money to ensure it does what you want it to do. Whether you are adding to your investments or depending on them soon, you always want to preserve them. Remember, risk is everywhere, including Treasury bills and your mattress; they all run the risk of losing buying power. Being in the bond or equity market also carries risk; there are no investment formulas that come without risk. The idea here is to always mitigate your risks and to be aware of them and when they are higher and lower. Like all investment strategies, a contrarian point of view will not be successful all of the time, but my hope is that you fully understand the decisions and strategies you are making with your investments.

The equity market has a much better chance of growing your capital as well as beating inflation if investments are made consciously, are continuously monitored, and vehicles for losses and gains are put in place. Because timing is paramount, you can test out the different indicators until you feel comfortable with them and then make changes or recommendations for change in your percentages. Remember, there is a time to buy and a time to sell.

There could easily be a 20, 40, or even a 60 percent correction over the coming few years; the risk is there. If you are concerned about the market at any time, use any of the ideas that were presented in the risk lesson. Be diversified. Be Flexible.

Just remember, there are always opportunities whether the market goes up or down.

Here is a list to get you started in the right direction.

1. Find an advisor who will work with you to help determine where you are, your future goals, and how you will implement them *together*.

2. Pay off high-interest debt even if you have to use low-interest debt to do so.

3. If you have children, start a Registered Education Savings Plan (RESP).

4. Maximize your Tax-Free Savings Account (TFSA).

5. Maximize your Registered Retirement Savings Plan (RRSP) and spousal RRSP. Your income-tax refund must be invested in a non-registered account to be used in later years to pay for the tax deferral that you received.

6. Look into a guaranteed whole life insurance policy for peace of mind and creditor protection.

7. Real estate is a great investment and could help immensely as far as income. Do not buy a second property hoping it will increase in value. Buy a second property to renovate or rent out. Make it a source of income, not a liability.

8. Depending on market timing, most of your investments should be in equities (be that long or short) because they have proven to outperform over almost any period of time. Be invested in the market only when the odds are on your side.

9. Be conscious of where your money is invested.

Be in bonds when interest rates are going down, not up. Use options and insured annuities to effectively reduce income tax.

Ignoring your investments and hoping for the best is not a good solution.

"Buy and hold" is not a good solution.

Having actively managed mutual funds is not a good solution.

Being aware, conscious, and involved works.

At the time of completing this book (December, 2014), I believe we are in a high-risk time for investing. I believe we are headed to a deflationary period, and the winter season for investing.

- Rates will stay low.
- China's growth is dead.
- Real estate prices will fall.
- US and Canadian equities will suffer losses.
- Commodity prices will further decrease.
- It will take at least three to five years to get over the demographic conundrum we are in.
- India will be the next leader coming out of this winter season.
- Be overly risk adverse in coming years. Hedge by being long and short the market and be prepared to prosper during the coming spring season of new growth.

Putting It All Together

I hope you have the fortitude to look at your investments and your future in a new light and begin to invest with confidence by

- redefining yourself;
- making a plan;
- saving *now*;
- understanding your investments;
- knowing the risks;
- being tax conscious; and
- picking a good advisor.

I hope that both my years in the investment industry and, more important, my thirteen years of retirement and reflection have provided new and innovative insight . This is not about following the crowd; rather, it is about being risk averse and involved. I hope this book pushes you to set new targets that, once implemented, will help you reach your goals. May you be one of the lucky ones to enjoy a secure, rewarding retirement and understand when enough is enough.

—Steve Renault

middleretirement.com.

ACKNOWLEDGMENTS

I would like to thank our friends Gina and Len for pushing me to stop ranting and begin this venture. To all those in the investment business who put faith in me throughout the years, their support guided my journey from floor trader to investment firm owner. Specifically, thank you to Mike Biscotti, Bob Dorrance, Jim Davidson, Frank Mersch, Barb Lee, Rick Crowe and Ron Smith, who gave me my first real opportunity.

To my mother for her lifelong devotion, caring, and inspiration and my father, whose wisdom continues to ring daily in my ears; I miss them dearly. To my sons Brandon, Caleb, Joshua and Levi, and daughter, Heather, who are always interested in debating an issue and listening to me work through my ideas.

To my wife, Lisa, thank you not only for your help and support on this book, but for being a life partner who is more faithful, honest and loving than anyone I know. You are the true inspiration and courage behind our life adventures and middle retirement.

NOTES

1. Economics Made Simple, Madsen Pirie, Page 7
2. Economics Made Simple, Madsen Pirie, Page 9
3. MoneyNews- February 13, 2013
4. Financial Post- October 11, 2013
5. Globe and Mail- November 15, 2013
6. Compiled by Imagin8ion Design
7. Wall Street Journal- October 3,2013
8. New York Times- October 17,2013

*Note: All charts and diagrams in this book have been designed and produced by

Imagin8ion Design.

GLOSSARY

Accredited Investor (High Net Worth)

Is a term defined by a country's securities laws that delineates investors permitted to invest in certain types of presumed higher-risk investments such as seed capital, limited partnerships, hedge funds, and private placements. In the United States as well as Canada, for an individual to be considered an accredited investor, he or she must have a net worth of at least $1 million, not including the value of his or her primary residence or have income of at least $200,000 each year for the last two years (or $300,000 together with his or her spouse if married).

Active Fund Manager (AFM)

Refers to a portfolio management strategy where the manager makes specific investments with the goal of outperforming an investment benchmark.

Annuity

A contract by which one receives fixed payments on an investment for a lifetime or for a specific number of years.

Asset

Is an economic resource. Anything tangible or intangible that is capable of being owned or controlled to produce value or has economic value (e.g., stocks, your education, real estate).

Asset Allocation

An investment strategy that attempts to balance risk versus reward by adjusting the percentage of each asset in an investment portfolio according to the investor's risk tolerance, goals, and investment time frame.

Asset Class

A group of economic resources sharing similar characteristics, such as risk and return (stocks are a separate asset class than are bonds).

Glossary

Bear Market

Is a general decline in the stock market over time. It is a transition from high investor optimism to widespread fear and pessimism. The generally accepted measure is a price decline in the overall index of 20 percent.

Bearish

A term used to describe investor sentiment when the investor expects downward price movement in an asset.

Benchmark

A standard against which the performance of a security, mutual fund, or investment fund can be measured. Generally a market segment, stock index, or bond index is used (e.g., Dow Jones Industrial Average [DJIA], Standard & Poor/Toronto Securities Exchange [S&P/TSX]).

Beta

The measure of volatility (risk) of an investment arising from exposure to general market movements. The overall market has a beta of 1. A stock with a .7 beta says it is less volatile than the market, whereas a stock with a beta of 1.7 says it has more volatility than the market. The securities regulators believe that volatility = risk.

Bond

A debt investment in which an investor loans money to an entity (corporate or government) that borrows the funds for a defined period at a fixed interest rate.

Brokerage Firm

Is a financial institution that facilitates the buying and selling of financial securities between buyers and sellers.

Budget

Is a quantitative expression of a plan for a defined period.

Bull Market

Is a period of generally rising prices. It is a transition period from pessimism to optimism and eventually euphoria.

Glossary

Bullish

A term used to describe investor sentiment when the investor expects rising price movements in an asset.

Business Cycle (Economic Cycle)

Refers to fluctuations in aggregate production, trade, and activity over several months or years in a market economy.

Buy and Hold Strategy

An investment strategy where an investor buys stocks or funds and holds them for long periods. It is based on the view that in the long run, financial markets give good rates of return despite declines in the markets.

Call Option (Calls)

Is a financial contract between two parties, the buyer and the seller. The buyer of the call option has the *right*, but not the obligation, to buy an agreed number of shares at a specific time for a specific price. The seller (writer) of the call has the *obligation* to sell those shares if the buyer so decides.

Capital Asset Pricing Model (CAPM)

A model that describes the relationship between risk and expected return and that is used in the pricing of risky securities. CAPM assumes that risk is equal to volatility.

Capital Gain

An increase in the value of a capital asset (investment or real estate) that gives it a higher worth than the purchase price. In Canada, capital gains are taxed at the lowest tax rate even after they are reduced by capital losses.

Contraction Phase

A phase of the business cycle in which the economy as a whole is in decline. More specifically, contraction occurs after a cycle peak and before a trough. This is a time to be invested in less-risky stocks such as utilities and consumer staples as well as in cash as opposed to equities in general. It is also a time to be purchasing bonds as interest rates tend to decrease.

Glossary

Contrarian

An investor who attempts to profit by investing in a manner that differs from conventional wisdom, when the consensus opinion appears to be wrong.

Corporate Finance

This division of an investment firm is responsible for advisory, debt (bonds) and equity (stocks) issuances, and mergers and acquisitions (M&A). Arguably the most profitable arm of a brokerage firm.

Covered Call Writing

A financial market transaction in which the seller of call options owns the corresponding amount of the underlying security (same number of shares). This is a great tool for adding income to a portfolio.

Derivatives

A special type of contract that derives its value from the performance of an underlying asset (e.g., options, futures, exchange-traded funds [ETFs]).

Deflation

Is a decrease in the general price levels of goods and services. Deflation occurs when the inflation rate falls below 0 percent. The inflation rate is determined by the Consumer Price Index (CPI).

Dividend

A payment made by a corporation to its shareholders, usually as a distribution of profits.

Earnings per Share (EPS)

The monetary value of earnings per each outstanding share of a company's common stock.

Economic Indicators

Is a statistic about an economic activity. Economic indicators allow analysis of economic performance and predicts future performance. Popular indicators are unemployment rates, housing starts, Consumer Price Index, retail sales, etc.

Efficient Market Hypothesis (EMH) (Theory)

Asserts that financial markets are "informationally efficient," and thus, one cannot consistently achieve returns in excess of the average market returns on a risk-adjusted basis.

Exchange-Traded Fund (ETF)

Is an investment fund traded on stock exchanges, much like stocks, yet are baskets of an asset class like a mutual fund. An ETF holds assets such as stocks, bonds, and commodities, and theoretically trades close to its net asset value of the underlying asset. They are tax efficient, liquid, and easy to buy or sell.

Financial Advisor

A professional who renders financial advice to clients.

Fundamental Analysis

Analyzing a business's financial statements and health of its management and its competitors and the markets. It focuses on debt, earnings, and productivity in order to make financial forecasts.

Goals

The desired result a person envisions. A goal is derived from planning. A goal needs a specific dollar amount and a specific time line to be obtainable.

Growth Phase

The phase in the economic cycle where corporate earnings and economy health is strengthening. This is the time to be fully invested in growth stocks.

Hedge Fund

An investment vehicle that pools capital from investors to invest in securities. Unlike a mutual fund which aims to outperform a benchmark, a hedge fund mandate is absolute returns.

Index Fund

An investment vehicle that aims to replicate the movements of a specific financial market or asset class.

Inflation

A sustained increase in the general price level of goods and services as measured by the Consumer Price Index (CPI).

Insured Annuity

Uses two products: a prescribed annuity and a life insurance policy. Because of deferred tax treatment of a prescribed annuity, the holder receives higher after-tax cash flow, resulting in a higher real return.

Interest Rate

The rate at which interest is paid by a borrower to the lender. Generally, the interest rate in Canada is referred to as the bank rate.

Inverse Exchange-Traded Fund (ETF)

An ETF traded on the public market that is designed to perform the inverse of the asset or index benchmark it is designed to track.

Investment

Putting money into an asset with the expectation of capital appreciation, dividends, and/or interest earnings.

Investment Industry Regulatory Organization of Canada (IIROC)

A nonprofit self-regulated organization that sets rules and investment industry standards for the Canadian investment community. The organization holds the power over compliance, registration, and hearings over firms and advisers. It is the highest regulatory body in Canada. Your adviser should be a member of this organization to ensure the highest standards in the industry.

Liability

Any asset that is borrowed (e.g., cash) that needs to be repaid or you are liable for (e.g., mortgage or rent).

Management Expense Ratio (MER)

A measure of what it costs an investment company to operate a mutual fund company (including salaries and profits).

Market Cycle

The period during which the stock market evolves from a bull market to a bear market, then back to a bull market (generally four years).

Market Timing

The strategy of making buy and sell decisions of financial assets (often stocks) by attempting to predict future market price movements.

Market Trend

A tendency of a financial market to have a particular direction over time.

Mutual Fund

A type of professionally managed investment product that pools money together from investors to purchase securities.

Mutual Fund Dealers Association (MFDA)

A Canadian self-regulatory organization that provides oversight to dealers and distributors of mutual funds (they do not regulate stocks, exchange-traded funds [EFTs], or any other investments).

Non-registered Account

A type of investment account that has no restrictions or limits, nor does it offer tax advantages as with a registered account.

On-Stop Order to Sell

An order placed with a broker to sell a security at a certain price. It is designed to limit potential investor loss, as well as to protect an investor's gain.

Optimal Diversification

The point of diversification that maximizes the quality of a portfolio without reducing the quality of the portfolio.

Option (Option Contract)

A contract that allows the holder to buy or sell an underlying security at a given price over a specified period.

Glossary

Overbought

A situation in which the demand for a certain asset unjustifiably pushes the price of the asset to high levels that do not support the fundamentals.

Oversold

A situation in which the supply for a certain asset unjustifiably pushes the price of the asset to low levels that do not support the fundamentals.

Passive Investing

An investment strategy involving limited buying and selling with the intent of long-term appreciation and limited maintenance (index funds are ideal for this strategy).

Peak

The highest point between the end of an economic expansion phase and the start of a contraction phase in a business cycle.

Pension Funds

A fund established by an employer to facilitate and organize the investments of employees' retirement fund contributions (e.g., Ontario Teachers Pension Fund).

Private Equity

An alternative investment using equity capital that is not quoted on a public exchange (private equity firms invest in new technologies, distressed companies, and start-ups).

Put Option (Put)

A stock market device that gives the buyer of the put the *right* to sell the underlying asset at a specified price for a specified period. The seller is obligated to buy the underlying shares if the owner of the put so desires.

Random Walk Theory

States that stock price changes are independent, and thus, past movements or stock price trends cannot be used to predict future moves.

Glossary

Registered Retirement Savings Plan (RRSP)

A type of Canadian savings and investing account with tax advantages that was introduced to promote savings for retirement.

Relative Strength

A technical momentum indicator that compares the magnitude of recent gains to recent losses in an attempt to determine overbought and oversold conditions.

Risk-Free Asset

An asset which has a certain future return. Treasuries are considered to be risk free because they are backed by the U.S. government.

Risk/Reward Ratio

A ratio used by investors to compare the expected returns of an investment to the amount of risk undertaken to capture these returns.

Short Sale (Sell Short)

A market transaction in which an investor sells borrowed securities in anticipation of a price decline and is required to return an equal number of shares at some point in the future.

Stock

A share of the stock of a company constitutes the equity stake of its owner (a piece of the company).

Tax-Free Savings Account (TFSA)

A Canadian savings and investing account that provides tax benefits for saving. Any gains on monies deposited is earned tax-free.

Technical Analysis

A method of evaluating securities by analyzing statistics generated by market activity such as price and volume.

Trough

The stage of the economic business cycle that marks the end of a period of declining business activity and the transition to the expansion phase.

Wealth

The abundance of valuable resources or material possessions.

Stephen Renault has been involved with the financial industry since 1982. Moving from floor trader to brokerage firm owner and then retiree to his career today as financial advisor to youth, seniors and mid lifers. Renault was born and raised in rural Ontario. He splits his time between Canada and the US.

middleretirement.com

CPSIA information can be obtained at www.ICGtesting.com
Printed in the USA
LVOW10s1033220815

451157LV00004B/349/P

9 781502 440013